Justice in Aboriginal Communities

Purich's Aboriginal Issues Series

Justice in Aboriginal Communities
Sentencing Alternatives

Ross Gordon Green

Purich Publishing
Saskatoon, Saskatchewan
Canada

All inquiries and orders regarding this publication should be addressed to:

Purich Publishing
Box 23032, Market Mall Postal Outlet
Saskatoon, SK
Canada S7J 5H3

Phone: (306) 373-5311   Fax: (306) 373-5315   Email: purich@sasktel.net
Website: www.purichpublishing.com

Canadian Cataloguing in Publication Data

Green, Ross Gordon, 1955–

Justice in aboriginal communities : sentencing alternatives

(Purich's aboriginal issues series)

Includes bibliographical references and index.
ISBN 978-189583010-1

1. Native peoples--Legal status, laws, etc.--
Canada.* 2. Sentences (Criminal procedure)--
Canada. 3. Alternatives to imprisonment--
Canada. I. Title. II. Series.

KE7722.C75 G74 1998   364.6'5'08997071 C98-920102-3
KF8210.C7 G74 1998

Editing, design, and layout by Page Wood Publishing Services, Saskatoon
Cover design by NEXT Communications, Inc., Saskatoon
Printed in Canada by Houghton Boston
Printed on acid-free paper

Fifth Printing 2014

Purich Publishing Ltd. gratefully acknowledges the assistance of the Government of Canada through the Canada Book Fund, and the Creative Industry Growth and Sustainability Program made possible through funding provided to the Saskatchewan Arts Board by the Government of Saskatchewan through the Ministry of Parks, Culture and Sport for its publishing program.

Printed on 100% post-consumer, recycled, ancient-forest-friendly paper.

 Canadian Heritage Patrimoine canadien  Government of Saskatchewan Ministry of Parks, Culture and Sport SASKATCHEWAN ARTS BOARD

Contents

Acknowledgements

I am grateful to many people for helping me with this book. My warmest thanks are reserved for my spouse, Brenda, my daughter, Margaret, and my son, Ian, for their love, support, and understanding during this project. I also thank my mother, Margaret, and my brother, Keith, for their help and support during our year spent in Winnipeg during my LL.M. studies.

The idea for this book came from my thesis for my Master of Laws degree. After completing my thesis in August 1995, I decided that I should expand the work to make it available to a broader audience. To do this, I added some new material and drew on my personal experiences as a defence lawyer. The area of criminal law sentencing is dynamic and has seen many changes over the past few years. This book considers recent changes to the sentencing provisions of the *Criminal Code* and recent court decisions that directly affect the evolution of the alternative approaches to sentencing I discuss.

I am grateful for the financial assistance I received from the Law Society of Saskatchewan (through the Culliton Scholarship) and from the University of Manitoba Faculty of Law (through the Freedman Graduate Fellowship), and for the research grants awarded to me through the University of Manitoba Legal Research Institute and the Government of Canada Northern Scientific Training Program. I wish to thank many people for their assistance in making my year in the Master of Laws program both exciting and rewarding. I am also grateful to Judge Eric Diehl of Melfort, Saskatchewan, and Dean Peter MacKinnon and Professor Beth Bilson, both of the College of Law at the University of Saskatchewan, for acting as referees on my application to the LL.M. program.

Within the Faculty of Law at the University of Manitoba, I am especially indebted to my supervisor, Professor Anne McGillivray, for her advice, encouragement, support, and patience throughout my year of study at that institution. I appreciate the commitment and assistance of my internal reader, Professor David Deutscher, and of Dr. DeLloyd Guth, Chair of Graduate Studies. Elsewhere at the University of Manitoba, I am indebted to my external reader, Professor Russell Smandych of the Department of Sociology, for his insight and kindness and for his significant contribution to my project. Many others from the Faculty of Law assisted me, including Professors Lee Stuesser, Trevor Anderson, Alvin Esau, Brian Schwartz,

Barney Sneiderman, Cam Harvey, Freda Steel, John Irvine, and Neil Campbell; Wendy Whitecloud, Director of the Academic Support Program; and law student Simon Helm. I also appreciate the help of the faculty's support staff, including Sue Law, Margaret Dufort, and Cheryl Hapko; and the assistance of the entire staff at the E. K. Williams Library, including Reference Librarian John Eaton, Reference Assistant Gail Mackisey, and Circulation Supervisor Susanne Wallace. On a personal level, I thank colleagues Tetsuya Aman and Ian Malkin for their support, advice, and companionship during my year at the University of Manitoba.

During my study at the University of Manitoba, I travelled to six Aboriginal communities in Manitoba and Saskatchewan. I received assistance, advice, and support from many people during my field work. In Saskatchewan, these people included Harry and Adelle Morin and Brian Brennan of Sandy Bay; Dorothy and Cyril Roy of Cumberland House; Judge Claude Fafard, Sid Robinson, and Robin Ritter of La Ronge; Gerry Morin and Earl Kalenith of Prince Albert; Judge Bria Huculak of Saskatoon; and the staff of the Legal Aid Area Office in Melfort (Barry Treacy, Brenda Dahlby, Lorraine Sebelius, Kathy Godson, and Gloria Tkachuk). In Manitoba, these people included Joyce Dalmyn and Judge William Martin of The Pas; Berma Bushie of Hollow Water; James Goertzen and Kathy Belaja of Dauphin; and Judge Murray Sinclair, Judge Robert Kopstein, and William Macdonald of Winnipeg. I also thank Judge Barry Stuart of Whitehorse, Yukon, and Rupert Ross of Kenora, Ontario, for their comments during my study. My final thanks are to Don Purich (publisher) and Jane Billinghurst (editor) of Purich Publishing for their substantial efforts in publishing my book.

With the exception of the photograph credited to the *Winnipeg Free Press,* I took all the photographs in this book during court sittings with the consent of the presiding judge.

Illustrations

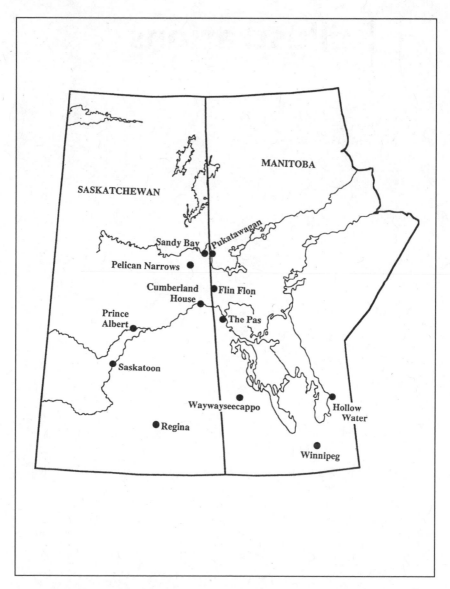

This book discusses innovative approaches to criminal sentencing and mediation that have evolved in Aboriginal communities, including sentencing circles at Hollow Water, Manitoba, and Sandy Bay, Saskatchewan; an elders' sentencing panel at Waywayseecappo, Manitoba; sentence advisory committees at Pelican Narrows and Sandy Bay, Saskatchewan; a community mediation committee at Pukatawagan, Manitoba; and a sentencing circle committee at Cumberland House, Saskatchewan, that functioned both as a sentence advisory committee and as a community mediation committee. This map shows the location of the communities studied, with larger urban centres noted for reference.

The road north to Sandy Bay, Saskatchewan. All the communities studied were isolated from larger urban centres to the south.

Main Street in Sandy Bay at 9:00 a.m. This community is served by a local detachment of the Royal Canadian Mounted Police. Typical cases coming before the court include break and enter, theft, and assault.

Members of the court party fly in to northern communities such as Sandy Bay once a month to hear cases and pronounce sentence. This arragement has raised feelings of estrangement from the court on the part of local residents and has resulted in requests for more local participation in the criminal justice system.

Court is held in Sandy Bay in the basement of this church. Court in northern communities is typically held in community halls that are otherwise used for social activities such as bingos and dances.

This photograph illustrates a conventional court setting in Sandy Bay, with the judge sitting at a table facing those in attendance. (April 19, 1995)

A sentencing circle in Sandy Bay for an offender who had plead guilty to assault. In this setup, all participants, including the offender, judge, victim, police, and assorted community members, sit in a circle facing each other. Participants try to agree on an appropriate sentence. Discussions usually focus on the causes of criminal behaviour and what resources can be accessed locally to reform and rehabilitate the offender. (April 19, 1995)

Members of the justice committee at the Mathias Colomb Cree Nation in Pukatawagan, Manitoba, sit with the judge at a sentencing hearing to advise on sentence. This committee was also involved with mediating offences and other disputes between community members outside of court. (April 1995)

This sentencing circle at Hollow Water First Nation, Manitoba, dealt with a man and a woman who had plead guilty to incest. It lasted twelve hours. After all in attendance had been allowed input, the offenders received a suspended sentence with conditions requiring sexual offendeer treatment at the local holistic treatment centre. (December 9, 1993. Kevin Rollason, *Winnipeg Free Press*, reprinted with permission)

Introduction

This book is about community participation in the sentencing of Aboriginal offenders in Aboriginal communities. It is also about finding alternatives to current sentencing practices both inside and outside of our courts. It was written in response to current concerns about the high level of incarceration of Aboriginal people tried in courts designed by the prevailing white justice system. The causes of Aboriginal over-incarceration in Canada in the 1990s are wide ranging and complex. Professor Tim Quigley of the University of Saskatchewan has suggested they include the poor socio-economic circumstances of many Aboriginals, the high percentage of Aboriginal youth within the range of age most susceptible to criminal activity, the level of policing in Aboriginal communities, the "snowball" effect of a prior criminal record, a greater likelihood of an Aboriginal accused being denied bail, and the lack of sentencing alternatives available for sentencing under the *Criminal Code*.[1]

Although concerns regarding sentencing law and practice form only a portion of the concerns expressed in Aboriginal communities about the Canadian justice system, new approaches to sentencing may form part of the solution to the problems encountered by Aboriginal offenders and their families. Clearly, there is enormous discretion available within the existing system to address these concerns. As Chief Justice Bayda of the Saskatchewan Court of Appeal stated in his dissenting judgement in *R. v. Morin:*

> [O]ur present justice system is flexible, accommodating and geared to do what must be done to achieve fairness and justice for all. That quality enables the system to embrace sentencing circles as part of the system and to ascribe to them a role in addressing the disparity in the prison population by empowering communities to help individuals break their personal cycles of misbehaviour.[2]

It is unrealistic to expect changes in sentencing practice alone to achieve a significant reduction in the incarceration rate of Aboriginal offenders; however, exploring sentencing alternatives for Aboriginal offenders is one way that the rate of incarceration for Aboriginal offenders in Canada might be reduced, and diversion of offenders from the court system to community mediation committees is another.

The need for sentencing reform within Aboriginal communities appears unquestionable, given the product of the conventional sentencing process. Professor Michael Jackson detailed the over-representation of Aboriginal people within Canadian jails and observed that "[m]ore than any other group in Canada they are subject to the damaging impacts of the criminal justice system's heaviest sanctions."[3] Jackson described the situation in Manitoba and Saskatchewan as particularly distressing, with Aboriginal people, while constituting only 6 to 7 percent of the population, representing 46 percent and 60 percent of the respective prison admissions.[4] Figures from Statistics Canada confirm the continuation of this over-representation. In 1993–94, Aboriginal persons constituted 71 percent and 47 percent of the admissions to provincial correctional centres in Saskatchewan and Manitoba.[5] Recently, the Royal Commission on Aboriginal Peoples stressed the disproportionate number of Aboriginal people going to jail and commented that the "over-representation of Aboriginal people in Canadian prisons has been the subject of special attention . . . because the sentence of imprisonment carries with it the deprivation of liberty and represents Canadian society's severest condemnation."[6]

The negative impact of jail upon First Nations offenders and communities was described by Chief Judge Lilles of the Yukon Territorial Court in *R.* v. *Gingell,* when he summarized the feelings of participants in that sentencing circle:

> Jail has shown not to be effective for First Nation people. Every family in Kwanlin Dun [the Yukon] has members who have gone to jail. It carries no stigma and therefore is not a deterrent. Nor is it a "safe place" which encourages disclosure, openness, or healing. The power or authority structures within the jail operate against "openness". An elder noted: "Jail doesn't help anyone. A lot of our people could have been healed a long time ago if it weren't for jail. Jail hurts them more and then they come out really bitter. In jail all they learn is "hurt and bitter".[7]

Allowing local communities to become more actively involved in the sentencing and supervision of offenders introduces a wider range of alternatives into the sentencing process. In contrast to the conventional sentencing hearing is the practice of circle sentencing, which has recently been employed by judges presiding in various Aboriginal communities across Canada. Although these circles are formed within the parameters of existing Canadian law, retaining for the judge discretion as to whether such a circle is formed and the ultimate sentencing decision, they allow significant opportunity for input from victims and local community members. In addition to making representations on their own behalf (as opposed to being represented by Crown or defence submissions), victims and local community members are allowed input in shaping, and potentially supervising, offender sentences. Community participation is not a panacea; however, taken together with the availability and provision of adequate treatment and professional resources within a community, such local input may create a real opportunity for beginning to break deviant cycles of behaviour among repeat offenders.

As a criminal defence lawyer practising in central Saskatchewan since 1986, and as a lecturer in the Criminal Procedure Section of the Law Society of Saskatchewan Bar Admission Course, I have spent the last decade immersed in the problems associated with the sentencing of Aboriginal offenders. In June 1993, I attended a conference of the Northern Justice Society in Kenora, Ontario. Several presentations focussed on the inadequacies of prevailing sentencing practices in Aboriginal communities and contained suggestions for reform. The ideas I heard expressed at the conference motivated me to do some research of my own. I subsequently conducted a detailed study of community sentencing and mediation in Aboriginal communities while completing my LL.M. degree at the University of Manitoba.

To analyse the various initiatives within the Aboriginal communities I studied, I came up with the following four models:

- the sentencing circle,
- the elders' or community sentencing panel,
- the sentence advisory committee, and
- the community mediation committee.

Although I consider each of these models individually in this book, the models are not mutually exclusive and a combination of approaches may exist within a community.

I undertook my study from September 1994 to August 1995. I studied sentencing circles at Hollow Water, Manitoba, and Sandy Bay, Saskatchewan; an elders' sentencing panel at Waywayseecappo, Manitoba; sentence advisory committees at Pelican Narrows and Sandy Bay, Saskatchewan; a community mediation committee at Pukatawagan, Manitoba; and a sentencing circle committee at Cumberland House, Saskatchewan, that functioned both as a sentence advisory committee and as a community mediation committee.

Part one of this book focusses on the often-tenuous relationship between Aboriginal communities and the conventional Canadian criminal justice system, especially with respect to the sentencing of Aboriginal offenders. Part two discusses several new approaches to dealing with Aboriginal offenders that have been attempted over the past few years. The focus of this discussion is on both the advantages and the dangers of enhanced participation by offenders, victims, and local community members in sentencing and mediation. Part three evaluates the development and progress of the various approaches and initiatives studied, and considers the implications these initiatives raise for reform of the justice system.

In the course of this discussion, it is important to keep in mind that the sentencing process is only a part of the overall criminal justice system. I believe that the most meaningful yardstick by which to judge the unconventional sentencing approaches outlined in this study is whether they provide an enhanced opportunity for changed offender behaviour, while at the same time allowing both local community participation and protection of victims. It is hoped that the revolving door between community and jail will, at the very least, be slowed through the new approaches to conventional justice practices examined in this book.

1 | Conventional and Aboriginal Systems of Justice and Sentencing Compared

1 | Sentencing Law and Practice in Canada

Criminal law in Canada is derived from the statutory and common law of England existing upon settlement of each territory.[1] These dates are September 17, 1792, for Ontario; October 1763 for Quebec; November 19, 1858, for British Columbia; July 15, 1870, for Manitoba, Alberta, Saskatchewan, the Northwest Territories, and the Yukon; and 1758 for Nova Scotia, New Brunswick, and Prince Edward Island. As a result of this historical link, current sentencing law and practice in Canada may largely be explained by considering the history of sentencing in English courts.

An English case from the late eighteenth century suggests a sentencing hearing similar to the process currently followed in most Canadian courts. The following passage from *R. v. Bunt* clearly suggests participation during sentencing was limited to the defence and Crown lawyers and to the judge:

> The defendants, who had been convicted of a conspiracy, were brought up for judgement on Friday, November the 14th; and it being disputed at the bar whether the counsel for the prosecutor or the prisoners should begin, the court thought it proper, in order to obviate the difficulty for the future which had perpetually occurred, to make a general rule for that purpose, without prejudicing the rights of the parties to this indictment. . . . [T]he court, after consideration, had resolved to adopt the following rule: when any defendant shall be brought up for sentence on any indictment, or information, after verdict, the affidavits produced on the part of the defendant . . . shall be first read, and then any affidavits produced on the part of the prosecution shall be read; after which the counsel for the defendant shall be heard, and lastly the counsel for the prosecution.[2]

The period following the Norman conquest of 1066 saw a gradual shift from a view of crime as a personal wrong (to be compensated by the offender, usually according to a fixed schedule of payments) to crime as a public wrong against all of society.[3] The emerging criminal system came to depend on the authority of the monarch and his or her agents.[4] As royal agents, judges came to exercise sole jurisdiction over sentencing. This power has continued to the present in both Canadian and English criminal law.[5]

The severity that characterized criminal law sentencing in England prior to the nineteenth century is striking. The number of capital crimes punishable by death increased from fifty to over two hundred between 1660 and 1820.[6] Perhaps in response to the perceived harshness of sentencing, the judicial practice of allowing convicted felons to make a speech in mitigation (in effect, a plea for their lives) was developed.[7] The death penalty could also be avoided by a convicted offender through application of benefit of clergy—the privilege exempting clergymen, or those claiming this status, from capital punishment[8]—or through a pardon from the monarch.[9]

Given the absolute role and authority of judges to impose sentence, the formal role of the local community in sentencing might appear to have been virtually non-existent. However, development of trial by jury,[10] which increased the community's role in fact-finding, also allowed jury members to influence offender punishment through a practice called "jury mitigation."[11] Perhaps moved by the severity of criminal law,[12] juries acted to mitigate punishment either by ignoring evidence and finding the accused not guilty,[13] or by finding the accused guilty of a lesser, non-capital charge, thereby avoiding capital punishment. One author described the practice by juries of finding a reduced value for items stolen so as to bring the offence within a classification not punishable by death.[14] This form of mitigation by the jury did not go unnoticed by judges, who imposed fines and imprisonment upon juries who "found against the evidence and the direction of the court."[15] Although such judicial retribution is unthinkable today, jury mitigation remains an example of community response to the perceived tyranny and misuse of power within the criminal courts of that earlier time.[16]

Some would argue that jury mitigation persists in current Canadian jurisprudence. In *Morgentaler* v. *R.*[17] the majority of the Supreme Court of Canada, in substituting a verdict of conviction for the jury's acquittal, criticized the lack of essential evidence to support such a verdict by the jury. In *R.* v. *Latimer*[18] the first trial jury, by returning a verdict of guilty to second- rather than first-degree murder, appeared to have employed a type of mitigation of penalty in the face of strong evidence at the trial to support planning and, hence, a conviction for first-degree murder.

The second trial jury in *R.* v. *Latimer*[19] clearly sought input into the decision on sentence. Prior to a verdict being returned, that jury asked the judge whether there was "any possible way" they could have input into a "recommendation on sentencing." Justice Noble of the Saskatchewan Court of Queen's Bench responded that they "were not to concern themselves with penalty." After the jury returned a verdict of guilty to second-degree murder, they went on to recommend that Robert Latimer have his parole eligibility set at one year rather than the prescribed minimum of ten years in section 745 of the *Criminal Code of Canada*. In a landmark decision, Justice Noble ruled that the minimum sentence prescribed by sections 235 and 745 of the

Code constituted cruel and unusual punishment for Latimer within the meaning of section 12 of the *Charter of Rights and Freedoms.* He then granted a constitutional exemption and sentenced Latimer to two years less a day, one half of which was to be served in the community as a conditional sentence of imprisonment. A significant factor in his decision on sentence appeared to be the actions taken by the jury.

The legal right of a convicted person to be represented by counsel prior to the passing of sentence did not occur until 1836, although prisoners facing felony charges were frequently allowed the assistance of counsel after 1730.[20] With the evolution of criminal law as a public wrong against society, the Crown prosecutor came to represent both the victim and the community in the sentencing process.

Whereas capital punishment was the central feature of criminal sentencing emerging from the eighteenth century both in England and what was to become Canada,[21] the nineteenth century saw significant reform of sentencing law and practice.[22] The death penalty was superseded first by transportation (the practice of sending an offender to a British colony either "as a condition for commuting a death sentence or as a penalty in its own right by the sentencing judge"[23]) and then by imprisonment as the major form of punishment. Consequently, by the mid-nineteenth century, judges had gained a significant increase in sentencing discretion.[24] This discretion initially focussed on the length of an offender's jail sentence.[25] The English *Consolidation Acts* of 1861,[26] largely copied in the Canadian *Consolidation Acts* of 1869,[27] established a statutory foundation for sentencing that remains intact today both in England[28] and in Canada, with high maximum penalties, broad judicial discretion, and few minimum penalties.[29] The sentencing options open to judges in England and Canada were further increased with the advent of probation early in the twentieth century.[30]

Nineteenth-century sentencing reforms were accompanied by concerns about sentencing disparities between judges[31] and by debates over appropriate principles of sentencing and purposes of punishment.[32] The predominant sentencing rationale emerging from the nineteenth century was deterrence: a belief that punishment would deter offenders from committing crimes, given the presumed "logical nature of man" to avoid painful consequences.[33] Deterrence remains a central theme of sentencing law in Canada and has been codified as an objective of sentencing in section 718(b) of the *Criminal Code.* Nineteenth-century justice reforms in England led to the overall codification of the criminal law, which had previously existed as a patchwork of disjointed statutory law together with the non-statutory common law. A draft English code prepared in 1879 by Sir James Fitzjames Stephen provided the basis of the Canadian *Criminal Code,* passed in 1892 by Parliament.[34]

The *Criminal Code* currently provides a range of sentencing options for most offences. A limited number of offences—such as impaired driving, using a firearm while committing an indictable offence, and murder—contain minimum penalties that restrict the range of sentencing options available. The potential sentences prescribed by the *Criminal Code* for most offences are a period of incarceration, which may be served in a prison or in the community subject to the terms of a conditional sentence order; a fine; a period of probation; or an absolute or conditional discharge. Conditional sentences of imprisonment are set out in section 742.1 of the *Code,* which allows the court to direct an offender to serve a sentence of imprisonment of less than two years in the community subject to the terms of a conditional sentence order. Such a sentence can be granted only when the judge is satisfied that "serving the sentence in the community would not endanger the safety of the community and would be consistent with the fundamental purpose and principles of sentencing set out in section[s] 718 to 718.2."[35]

The *Code* defines offences as summary (punishable by a maximum prison term of six months or, for some offences, eighteen months and/or a $2,000 fine), as indictable (punishable by a maximum prison term as prescribed for each offence and/or an unlimited fine), or as dual (punishable either as a summary or as an indictable offence). In the case of a dual offence, the Crown elects whether to proceed summarily or by indictment. This election governs both the maximum sentence and the trial process—most notably whether the accused is allowed a choice of trial by superior or provincial court.

The *Young Offenders Act*[36] provides a range of sentences, called dispositions, for young persons, who are defined as being at least twelve years but less than eighteen years of age. These dispositions are defined in section 20 of the act and include an absolute or conditional discharge, payment of restitution to a victim, a personal service order, community service work, a probation order, either secure or open custody, and any other conditions deemed reasonable by the court. An overall disposition may include a combination of these options so long as no inconsistency arises. With the exception of murder or any offence with a maximum sentence of life under the *Criminal Code,* a disposition for one offence may not exceed two years, while more than one offence can result in a total disposition of three years.[37]

Most offences defined by the *Criminal Code* provide for a maximum prison term without mention of a minimum sentence. As a result, judges are given enormous discretion in arriving at a fit sentence. A community-based sentence allows an offender to serve his or her sentence in the community rather than going to jail. Such a sentence often includes a probation order. The *Criminal Code* requires that a probation order be imposed in addition to a suspended sentence (which allows the court to re-sentence an offender if he or she commits another offence during the probation period), to a fine, or to a period of incarceration. The *Young Offenders Act* allows probation to be imposed alone or together with other dispositions.

Probation orders may remain in effect for up to three years under the *Criminal Code* and for up to two years under the *Young Offenders Act.* They require offenders to keep the peace and be of good behaviour and to report to the court if and when required. These orders may also include a variety of other conditions usually focussed on supervision and rehabilitation.

An adult offender awaiting sentencing for an offence without a minimum penalty and with a maximum punishment of less than fourteen years' imprisonment may be discharged, absolutely or conditionally, if the court finds such a disposition to be in the best interests of the accused and not contrary to the public interest. Such a discharge deems the accused not to have been convicted of the offence.

This range of sentencing options places great significance upon the sentencing hearing as this hearing is arguably the best opportunity to gather information about both the offender and the offence and, hence, to mould an appropriate sentence.[38] The information deemed relevant to a sentencing hearing may depend upon the offence committed and the sentencing principle deemed appropriate for this offence and offender. Community-based sentences are supported by the presentation of information confirming the availability of support, treatment, and supervision resources within the offender's community.

In ensuring a proper exercise of discretion at sentencing, the application of appropriate principles of sentencing to each case becomes critical. For example, the Saskatchewan Court of Appeal in *R.* v. *Morrissette*[39] recognized deterrence (both personal and general), punishment, protection of the public, and rehabilitation as significant sentencing principles. These principles are frequently cited at sentencing.

With amendment of the *Code* in September of 1996, section 718 now defines the fundamental purpose of sentencing as a respect for law and "the maintenance of a just, peaceful and safe society." This is to be achieved by imposing just sanctions that have one or more of the following objectives: denunciation of unlawful conduct, specific and general deterrence, incarceration of offenders where necessary, offender rehabilitation, victim and community compensation, and promotion of responsibility for and acknowledgement of harm done by offenders. Although these principles and objectives appear to be straightforward, the means by which they are to be achieved are not clear and have fostered considerable public and judicial debate. In particular, the role of incarceration in achieving any or all of these sentencing objectives has been questioned. In *R.* v. *McLeod,*[40] the efficacy of imprisonment as a means of achieving deterrence was questioned by Justice

Vancise of the Saskatchewan Court of Appeal. He commented that "[t]here is no empirical evidence that general deterrence as it relates to length of sentences is effective in reducing the crime rate" and that "[t]here is no evidence that higher sentences are effective in reducing the crime rate."

Public debates over sentencing policy and practice evidence many different viewpoints on how public safety can best be achieved. In the mainstream justice system, much emphasis is placed on punishment as a means of achieving safer communities. Jail is seen as the most effective tool in achieving this goal. Many Aboriginal people interviewed during the course of this study put forward perspectives on justice that showed a greater emphasis on healing and reconciliation and on finding alternatives to jail. The following chapter considers these perspectives in an historical context.

2 | An Historical Overview of Aboriginal Perspectives on Justice

In the course of this study, I analysed various sentencing initiatives that encouraged community, victim, and offender participation in Aboriginal communities. The communities I visited in Manitoba and Saskatchewan were of Cree and Ojibway descent. The Cree communities were Sandy Bay, Pelican Narrows, and Cumberland House[1] in Saskatchewan and Pukatawagan in Manitoba. The Ojibway communities were Hollow Water and Waywayseecappo in Manitoba. Given the heritage of these communities, my consideration of traditional dispute-resolution practices and their cultural evolution focusses primarily on the Cree and Ojibway people.

The Cree and Ojibway residing in Manitoba and Saskatchewan are descendants of woodland Indians who, prior to the arrival of Europeans in North America, resided in dense boreal forest regions across an enormous area of what is now Quebec, Ontario, and the prairie provinces.[2] Substantial migration of both the Cree and Ojibway took place after contact with Europeans through the fur trade, with the Cree moving west towards the prairies and the Ojibway migrating north towards James Bay.[3] These woodland tribes were nomadic hunters and gatherers who fed and clothed themselves by hunting moose, deer, bear, beaver, and caribou.[4] They mostly travelled in small family groups, although when food was plentiful in the summer they would come together in large numbers for feasts and religious ceremonies.[5]

Little, if any, autohistorical documentation exists respecting Cree and Ojibway culture prior to European contact in the early seventeenth century.[6] The body of written material on the traditional dispute-resolution practices of Aboriginal people represents interpretations by non-Aboriginals based on personal observations or discussions with elders. The problems in analysing traditional dispute-resolution practices are compounded by the dynamic nature of culture. Practices recognized and adopted within a culture depend to a great extent on current reality,[7] and traditions may be adapted or invented in response to such reality. Judge Claude Fafard of the Provincial Court of Saskatchewan, when questioned whether circle sentencing represented an appeal to tradition, commented that this approach might more accurately be described as "inventing" tradition.[8] Ultimately, it is the beliefs about tradition and the understanding and application of traditional practices within a culture that are significant. Colonization has eroded retention of traditional knowledge among First Nations in Canada.[9] The extent of this erosion, in conjunction with the historical development of each community, influences the similarity between current and historical practices.

The Aboriginal Justice Inquiry of Manitoba (AJI) summarized the existence and form of law in Aboriginal communities prior to contact with Europeans in the following terms:

> Law in an Aboriginal community was found in unwritten conventions before the arrival of Europeans. Although these rules were never codified, we observe that there were consistent patterns in the treatment of such matters as relations with other nations, family problems, and disputes about behaviour and property. These patterns became part of Aboriginal oral tradition and were passed from generation to generation. One can easily speak about these patterns in terms of "law" and "justice."[10]

Anthropologist Diamond Jenness described pre-contact law and order among tribes, including the woodland Cree and Ojibway, as depending "solely on the strength of public opinion" and being based on "rules and injunctions handed down by word of mouth from an immemorial antiquity."[11] He further observed that "persuasion and physical force were the only methods of arbitrating disputes, social outlawry or physical violence the only means of punishing infractions of the moral code or offences against the welfare of the band or tribe."[12] His account was criticized by the AJI commissioners,[13] who stated it reflected "cultural biases and stereotypes" about Aboriginal people prevalent during the 1930s. Despite this criticism,[14] the work of Jenness and others confirms that pre-contact Aboriginal societies clearly exercised an identifiable system of dispute resolution and social control. The AJI concluded that "[c]rime and punishment became part of each Aboriginal group's oral record, preserved by elders in story and legend."[15]

Both Cree and Ojibway societies were characterized by "community decision making . . . [as] a horizontal process which involved the participation and consent of the community at large"[16] and by generally informal social structures.[17] One author commented that, prior to signing treaties with the Canadian government in the late nineteenth century, the Ojibway had "no chiefs in the modern sense, nor any formal band or tribal organization."[18] The AJI painted the following picture of Cree and Ojibway justice practices:

> Ojibway and Cree cultural decision making involved the participation and consent of the community at large. Behaviour was regulated by ostracism, shame and compensation for the victim's loss, even if only symbolic compen-

sation were possible. Elders undertook the regular teaching of community values and warned offenders on behalf of the community. They publicly banished individuals who persisted in disturbing the peace. Elders might undertake to mediate dangerous disputes and to reconcile offenders with victims. In cases of grave threats or such serious offenses as murder, physical punishment and even execution of the offender might be undertaken either by the community or by those who had been wronged. In all instances the sanction of tribal elders was necessary.[19]

Such traditional methods of social control appear to have focussed on deterring crime through internal community pressure and sanction. Deterrence also constitutes a central goal of conventional Canadian sentencing policy,[20] although in the conventional justice system deterrence is often linked more directly to incarceration.

The role of traditional social-control mechanisms in deterring anti-social behaviour among the Cree and Ojibway of northwestern Ontario has been described by Rupert Ross, a Crown prosecutor and author from Kenora, Ontario:

> In traditional times, such deterrence was accomplished without much man-directed intervention. In the first place, the social group was the extended family, with the result that any harm done was harm to family members. Secondly, Mother Nature was the great enforcer, for anti-social conduct almost by definition diminished the capacity of the group to maintain bare survival in the woods. If man failed, Mother Nature punished. The overriding threat was banishment from the group, banishment into the wilds where, without the help of others, there was every likelihood of death. It was critical to each person that he maintain the welcome of the group, for without it he was lost.[21]

Ross also stressed the role of gossip in traditional social control.[22] Similarly, historian John Milloy described the practice of mocking and teasing as a means of encouraging conformation to social customs among the Plains Cree.[23]

Among pre-contact Cree, less serious offences such as theft and damage to property were treated as matters between offender and victim (or between their respective families), with an emphasis on compensating the victim. Anthropologist David Mandelbaum commented that, within traditional Plains Cree society, "[t]heft was rare and was usually the consequence of a thoughtless act by a young man" and that "[w]hen a boy's father discovered that a boy had taken something belonging to another, the parent would immediately return it to the owner."[24] Agnes Morin, an elderly Cree from Sandy Bay, put a similar emphasis on victim compensation:

I'll tell you a little story about myself when we were staying with my grand-parents. I was mischievous. And when we were staying with my uncles, my uncle, my dad they had everything, guns, snowshoes, and one day I decided to take my uncle's snowshoes and go in the bush. I didn't know how to walk around in snowshoes but I took them anyway. And I went in the bush and I said "I got snowshoes!" I got stuck in the snow and . . . I had this axe. I was going to chop a little stick to play with. . . . I chopped the snowshoe right in half and that was a very big thing and I knew I was in big trouble. I came home and I hid that snowshoe, my uncle's snowshoe. A few days after, my uncle said, "Well, it's a nice day. I'm going hunting." He looks for his snowshoes and I didn't say anything. I knew I would get into trouble. Finally, he found the snowshoes and one was cut in half with the axe. I was the only one there to be blamed, so my dad asked me, "Well, what did you do?" So, I told him I accidentally chopped it. And they were really mad. Really mad. . . . So my dad told my uncle, "Here's my snowshoes and I'll fix your snow-shoe while you're gone." My dad worked about two days to repair that snowshoe I broke. [I] never did that again.[25]

As the most serious of offences, murder within Cree and Ojibway society often resulted in revenge killings by the victim's family.[26] This blood vengeance was sometimes avoided through negotiation and compensation by the offender to the family of the deceased.[27] One historian wrote of the Plains Cree that if "a man murdered his wife through jealousy, as sometimes happened, he had to pay eight horses to his wife's relatives."[28] Banishment was another traditional sanction for such offences as murder. Chief Justice Bayda of the Saskatchewan Court of Appeal in *R.* v. *Taylor*,[29] in considering the propriety of a probation condition prescribing banishment of the offender to a remote island, commented that "First Nations people, including the Plains Cree and Dene, have for centuries used banishment in one form or another as a method of redress for a wrongdoing, particularly serious wrongdoing such as murder." Chief Justice Bayda went on to note that, unfortunately, there is a scarcity of literature on the subject.[30]

The traditional role of community circles in dispute resolution among the pre-contact Cree and Ojibway is difficult to assess. Given the limited size of nomadic hunting communities and the non-interventionist traditions of pre-contact woodlands tribes, it appears doubtful that community circles, similar in format and size to the sentencing circles currently being conducted, were used to facilitate dispute resolution. A study of the traditional practices of northwestern Ontario Cree described the family unit as the major deter-minant of dispute resolution and social control as a whole.[31] However, evidence does exist of community consultation following a transgression within traditional Cree and Ojibway society.[32] The use of circles appears to be accepted as having traditional significance by present-day Cree and Ojibway. Berma Bushie, co-ordinator of Community Holistic Circle Healing (CHCH) at Hollow Water First Nation in Manitoba, commented on Ojibway tradition:

> [T]he circle has a very significant role in our traditional way of life. Our whole culture is based on the circle. You look at the cycle of life, it's all in a circle, seasons are all in a circle. Everything! Everything operates on a circle in our culture. And this is what we have to return to. And definitely, in our work, the circle gives us the strength to be able to deal with these horrific cases [of sexual abuse].[33]

Verna Merasty, a Cree involved in healing and sentencing circles at Sandy Bay, confirmed the traditional role of circles within Cree culture.[34]

The lives of the Cree and Ojibway were significantly affected during the fur-trade era of 1660 to 1870.[35] During this period, Aboriginal people interacted with both French and English traders during expansion of the fur industry, often in co-operative fashion. As a significant force in shaping economic and political changes during this period, the fur trade required collaboration for the mutual benefit of Aboriginal people and European traders. With the ever-increasing exchange of furs for goods and supplies, neither party would have benefitted economically through elimination of the other.[36]

As a result of this interaction, Aboriginal people experienced significant cultural change.[37] Dispute resolution, previously controlled within each band, increasingly came to be controlled by colonizers. In the area of Rupert's Land, comprising most of current-day Manitoba and Saskatchewan, power was exerted by the Hudson's Bay Company (HBC). Despite ongoing debates in Upper Canada and in England regarding the scope and effect of the HBC charter and the applicable criminal law, a private justice system was created and enforced by HBC employees operating trading posts in this territory. Although research on this separate and often-harsh legal system has only just begun, sociologists Russell Smandych and Rick Linden have suggested that this system of private justice had a considerable impact on Aboriginal people.[38] Aboriginal people developed "many different creative strategies for dealing with European colonizers," some of which involved violence.[39] An example of a violent response by the Home Guard Cree of James Bay was noted by historian Paul Thistle, who described the destruction of Fort Henley by the Cree as a result of a perceived breach of reciprocal social obligations by HBC employees.[40] The Cree had been denied free entrance to the trading post, despite their understanding that this was the exchange for allowing Cree women to marry HBC employees.

Despite their resistance and efforts to the contrary, by mid-nineteenth century Aboriginal people in western Canada had seen their traditions, culture, and methods of dispute resolution encroached upon to a great extent by the influence and practices of the HBC.[41] Dispute resolution in and around the trading posts was controlled by colonial fur traders. No single law enforcement system existed during this era. The AJI observed:

> None of these incidents [examples of "rough justice"] should be seen as evidence of a consistent pattern of law enforcement. Instead, as one might conclude from Paul Thistle's detailed study of the Cumberland House district, the Indians lived according to their rules, and the fur traders by theirs within the context of company discipline. Moments of disagreement in Indian-European relations sometimes were resolved by force, sometimes not.[42]

Confusion was reported among nineteenth-century Europeans as to which colonial body—the courts of eastern Canada, on the one hand, or the HBC (by virtue of its power to enact laws for the good government of its territory), on the other—had jurisdiction over criminal offences in Rupert's Land.[43] The AJI commissioners argued that, despite the arrival of the Europeans, Aboriginal people never relinquished control over dispute resolution within their communities.[44]

Sale by the HBC of its interest in Rupert's Land to the Dominion of Canada in 1870 resulted in further colonization of Aboriginal people within this territory. Changes included negotiation of treaties, establishment of reserves,[45] and expansion of colonial criminal law enforcement into Aboriginal communities through the North-West Mounted Police, later the Royal Canadian Mounted Police (RCMP). Aboriginal land in the prairie region was ceded to the federal government through treaties made between 1871 and 1879. The results of this arrangement were both catastrophic and irreversible. Author Allan McMillan commented that "[i]n only a few decades these people had gone from proud and self-sufficient nomads, roaming freely across the Plains, to destitute and dependent groups, confined to small areas of land without any adequate means of support."[46]

In addition to the police presence, colonization of the Aboriginal population was enhanced through passage of federal legislation that came to regulate virtually all facets of life in Aboriginal communities. The AJI stated:

> The new justice system, as represented by the *Indian Act* and supplementary legislation, soon was being employed to prevent Aboriginal people from expressing their traditional beliefs, from pursuing their traditional economy and from asserting their political rights as individuals or as members of

Canadian society. In every aspect of life, from criminal law to education and religious expression, from hunting to agriculture, from voting to the use of lawyers, Aboriginal people ran into regulations that restricted their freedom.[47]

The move to reserve life meant a significant change in inter-community dynamics and dispute resolution. Life within multi-family reserves, often in excess of a thousand inhabitants, provided a proliferation of new relationships and an added complexity of life and potential for conflict outside the extended family.[48]

Although evidence points to the continued existence of distinct traditions of dispute resolution in Aboriginal communities, it is the conventional Canadian justice system that exerts control over criminal law enforcement and sentencing in these areas. How Aboriginal peoples perceive this imposed system and its powers of dispute resolution provides insights into potential change and reform of the existing system.

3 | Aboriginal People and the Canadian Justice System

"At the most basic level of understanding, justice is understood differently by Aboriginal people," wrote the AJI:

> The dominant society tries to control actions it considers potentially or actually harmful to society as a whole, to individuals or to the wrongdoers themselves by interdiction, enforcement or apprehension, in order to punish harmful or deviant behaviour. The emphasis is on the punishment of the deviant as a means of making the person conform, or as a means of protecting other members of society.[1]

The purpose of a justice system in an Aboriginal society is to restore peace and equilibrium within the community, and to reconcile the accused with his or her own conscience and with the individual or family that has been wronged. This is a primary difference. It is a difference that significantly challenges the appropriateness of the present legal and justice system for Aboriginal people in the resolution of conflict, the reconciliation of offenders and victims, and the maintenance of community harmony and good order.[2]

I frequently encountered perspectives supporting this interpretation of Aboriginal justice within the communities studied. Initially I thought the criticisms of the conventional justice system simply reflected a deep distrust and rejection of that system and were a sign of anger against it. Later, however, I saw these criticisms as more likely reflecting a fundamental difference in the meaning of justice and the process to be followed upon a offender's transgression. A recurrent theme was the replacement of the punitive focus of conventional Canadian law with a more conciliatory approach that emphasized the restoration of peaceful relations between offender, victim, and community. This view was reflected in the comments of Harry Morin, a Cree from Sandy Bay, who was active in the development of circle sentencing within his community:

> Like a lot of times, to me personally, the system is right now just a punishing system, it's punishing. They're not looking at what's causing these problems, they're looking at, hey, we have to punish this guy for what he's done, basically,

that's all it's at. And a lot of these guys go to jail, and they sit around this ten-by-twelve cell or whatever size they may be, and they sit there and think. And they get very bitter. [The offender's] bitter at the people that put him in there, the victim that reported him. He's mad at the justice system, he's mad at the RCMP. Here in a sentencing circle, we make sure somebody tells the offender that we're here to help, for support, and not only that, if recommendations are made that he takes some kind of programming to better himself back in society, he's not only promising to the magistrate or the probation officer, he's promising it to his own community. And then he knows he's got all that support.[3]

The Hollow Water assessment team also articulated a justice process that stands in sharp contrast to the conventional adversarial system:

[W]e are attempting to promote a process that we believe is more consistent with how justice matters would have been handled traditionally in our community. Rather than focussing on a specific incident as the legal system does at present, we believe a more holistic focus is required in order to restore balance to all parties of the victimization. The victimizer must be addressed in all his or her dimensions—physical, mental, emotional, spiritual—and within the context of all of his or her past, present, and future relationships with family, community, and Creator. The legal system's adversarial approach does not allow this to happen.[4]

Closely related to the perspective that questions the overall focus of the system is a sense of estrangement between local community members and the conventional justice system. This sense of estrangement is shared by many Aboriginal people and is reflected in the report of a 1988 Cree justice symposium in northern Quebec:

Whether because of being historically obliged to do so or whether in a certain way they accept it, owing to fate or the fact of its usefulness, the Cree communities have relied for almost a half century on a Western system of justice. In court a Cree has to answer only very indirectly to his own society; he is more answerable to a little known world, to a society foreign to his habits and traditions. And what is more, the society that bears the social costs of the transgression by that individual has neither control over that individual nor any say in the judicial process.[5]

Despite this sense of estrangement, the goals of Aboriginal and Canadian justice are similar. Members of the Indigenous Bar Association suggest that those similarities include deterrence of members from misconduct, public condemnation of offenders, restoration of the offenders to society, and punishment, if necessary.[6]

Although a plurality of views on justice is evident among Aboriginal people, there is significant emphasis on holistic approaches to justice that integrate the social, religious, and economic functioning of the offender vis-à-vis the community.[7] The Law Reform Commission of Canada recognized this and commented that "[t]he Aboriginal vision of justice gives pre-eminence to the interests of the collectivity, its overall orientation being holistic and integrative."[8] Similarly, the Task Force on the Criminal Justice System and Its Impact on the Indian and Metis People of Alberta commented that "[j]ustice and dispute resolution in traditional aboriginal societies can be illustrated by a restorative model of justice. . . . The holistic context of an offence is taken into consideration including moral, social[,] economic, political and religious considerations."[9]

Many Aboriginal dispute-resolution traditions and perspectives appear at odds with those accepted within the conventional Canadian justice system. Despite a common aim of controlling and deterring deviant behaviour and thereby protecting the community, Aboriginal justice approaches are characterized more by private inter- and intra-familial solutions, collective decision making, and an emphasis on reconciliation between offender, victim, and community, and less by an emphasis on punishment, the conventional Canadian approach.

The following section considers how such differences in perception and tradition, together with other factors, have affected conventional sentencing practices in Aboriginal communities.

The Circuit Court as Absentee Justice System

Most non-urban Aboriginal communities across Canada are serviced by circuit courts. Based in central urban locations, circuit court parties travel to these communities by road in the south and (usually) by air in the north. The northern fly-in court party usually comprises the judge, court clerk, Crown prosecutor, and legal aid counsel. Don Avison,[10] a former Crown counsel in the Yukon, described the often-tenuous relationship between the circuit court party and the community:

> I have strong memories of how difficult it was to get people to come to court there, even those who were actual parties to the disputes. I remember days in Carmacks, and other Yukon communities, when I was there in court trying to sort out what the appropriate response or sentence should be, knowing that I was part of a group of three—the judge, the prosecutor and the defence lawyer—who probably knew less about what had happened than anyone else

in the community, and we were the ones there to decide what the consequence should be. I also remember many times when I heard a dull rumble of voices behind me and I would know that, somehow, I had just fouled up the facts and there was no way to fix it.[11]

Many Aboriginal offenders facing sentence at circuit courts are intimidated by the process. Derek Custer and Cecile Merasty, two members of the sentencing circle committee at Pelican Narrows, Saskatchewan, explained that local offenders understand neither court procedures nor the English language. As a result, they usually stand mute before the judge, hoping their sentencing will be expedited.[12] This sense of confusion and intimidation has also been described by defence counsel Nick Sibbeston of the Northwest Territories, who commented that "[t]he general impression Dene people have of the court circuit is that a bunch of strangers, most of whom are non-native people, have come to town." He said these people "see the court proceedings as very strict and formal, and for most of them, scary."[13] Estrangement from the circuit court system was also evident in the comments of Harry Morin from Sandy Bay:

> With the probation officer or the magistrate [the judge] . . . you only see him once a month. You don't care. You know, "I'll get away with this, I'll get away with that. They're not going to know." Well, of course, nobody knows because they're gone. Nobody sees them until the next court date. Here, he [the offender] knows the people that are involved, and he knows the people that care and they keep an eye [on him], and they tell him that right in the circle, "If you ever need any help, if you need someone to talk to, if something's troubling you, we're available." And if you don't have a phone, you know, and a lot of times the probation officers won't accept a collect call, what do you do? When the pressure gets so tough, do you just say, "To hell with it?" Well, basically, that's what the system is doing. Here, [in Sandy Bay] you have your community of people. You know who is there. You know who you can talk to.[14]

I frequently encountered such feelings of estrangement in the communities I studied.

Many problems have been associated with the administration of justice by non-resident circuit courts. These include large court dockets, time constraints, lack of interpreters for Aboriginal offenders, and cultural differences between court personnel and Aboriginal offenders and communities.[15] In northern Saskatchewan and Manitoba, circuit courts regularly face heavy case loads. For example, despite an extremely high case count, Sandy Bay is allocated only one court date per month. Constable Brian Brennan indicated

Sandy Bay had the second highest case load per member in Saskatchewan, next to La Loche. He reported that Sandy Bay had a total yearly load of nine hundred cases, shared by three officers who functioned without secretarial staff.[16]

Sentencing hearings in such communities are often conducted quickly with little participation by offenders, victims, and local community members. During my appearances in the courts of central Saskatchewan, I have often experienced days on which more than fifty Aboriginal accused have appeared. As the vast majority of these accused either entered guilty pleas or were found guilty, there was little time to consider offenders as individuals during sentencing. This case-processing approach has been described by Judge Fafard:

> I'm really not interested in making more sausage or better sausage or adding spice to the sausage. Personally, I want to see a change away from that. I want to see us do good work. I sometimes feel it doesn't really matter if I do the forty or fifty cases before me on the docket in the morning, because if I do get them all done, I will not have done them very well. If I could do just a few of them and do them well, I would probably be further ahead than having case-processed them all and having done a bad job. So what we have at the moment, I believe, is an offender-processing system. It's not a criminal justice system because we're not achieving justice. We're not resolving the conflicts and the problems that are brought to us, and I think that our present system, as we operate it, just doesn't have the wherewithal to do that.[17]

Given current restraints on public funding in all sectors of government, a significant increase in court resources to allow for the additional time and personnel required to move away from a case-processing system appears unlikely. The more likely scenario is that we shall see incremental changes to conventional sentencing practice based on the requests and advocacy of lawyers or lay community members or on the willingness of judges to take risks and depart from the status quo.

A further explanation of the seeming detachment displayed by Aboriginal offenders at conventional sentencing is that facing a judge is viewed as simpler than facing one's own community. This view was echoed in comments made by Constable Brian Brennan of Sandy Bay, who explained differences between conventional sentencing and circle sentencing:

> And it really actually confronts the accused a lot more . . . standing . . . before his community, and admitting that he was wrong and explaining why he did it, than to stand before a stranger. It's easier to stand before a stranger for four to five minutes while the judge sentences you and be done with it, than to

sit for an hour or two, maybe even three, and have a number of people criticize your character and your actions, and you have to try to defend yourself.[18]

These comments reflect the impact of local systems of social control on offender response, and confirm the status of circuit court judges and personnel as "strangers" and "outsiders."

The relative isolation of rural and northern communities may be a factor in the relationship between the court and the community. Local participants and resources may be more easily identified and accessed in northern Aboriginal communities that are geographically isolated from the larger centres of the South and whose population is generally less transient. Constable Brennan associated community isolation and population stability with the availability of the local support systems he viewed as prerequisite to effective circle sentencing. He contrasted the situation in Sandy Bay with that of the Red Earth and Shoal Lake Reserves, 250 kilometres (155 miles) to the south, where he had been stationed previously:

> The main difference is that Sandy Bay is an isolated community. . . . I think sentencing circles can work in any community anywhere if there's the proper support structure. I don't think that in a place like Red Earth and Shoal Lake unless that support structure's there . . . that it's going to work. They're [the residents of Red Earth and Shoal Lake] on the move. They move back and forth between Nipawin and the reserves and Prince Albert . . . so much that you don't have the solid core community support that you need to have a sentencing circle work.[19]

Although time constraints and separation from local communities and local culture are problems faced by circuit courts sitting in Aboriginal communities, one advantage appears to be the broader discretion over the sentencing process exercised by circuit court judges in comparison with urban judges. A significant majority of the sentencing circles conducted in Saskatchewan by the fall of 1997 had been conducted by northern judges operating out of La Ronge and Meadow Lake. During a sentencing circle on April 19, 1995, at Sandy Bay,[20] Judge Fafard estimated that he had conducted between sixty and seventy sentencing circles. In addition, Judge Bria Huculak and Judge Ross Moxley, both previously of La Ronge, and Judge Jeremy Nightingale of Meadow Lake had been active in conducting sentencing circles in northern Saskatchewan. Judge Huculak stated unequivocally that circle sentencing development in northern Saskatchewan had been essentially "judge driven."[21]

The tendency of northern circuit judges to depart from conventional practice is not new. This is reflected in the following description of a 1978 court hearing conducted by Judge Jim Slaven of the Territorial Court of the Northwest Territories:

> The court party arrived in Rankin by plane from Yellowknife at noon on the trial date. It was an autumn day in 1978 and Judge Slaven was ready to proceed. But a group of Rankin people—Inuit—asked him to delay proceedings. They were calling a community meeting to talk about the young man [the accused] and his fate. "It was the first time that such a thing had happened in Rankin," the judge said, "the first time the local people had ever sat down together. You see, coming from all various backgrounds the way they had, different strains of Eskimo, they'd never merged as a real community. There was a professor up there, fellow named Williamson from the University of Saskatchewan, who'd been going to Rankin for eighteen years, and he said this was the old traditional Inuit way of doing things, meeting together and looking after their own. Well, hell, under those circumstances the court was pleased to stand aside for a few hours. That might sound ridiculous to [a] judge in the south but northern justice is different.[22]

This breadth of judicial discretion allowed innovation by individual judges to significantly affect the relationship between court and community. Greg Bragstad, a participant in several sentencing circles at Sandy Bay, commented on the local impact of Judge Fafard:

> Judge Fafard I find, anyway, has made a tremendous impact here and has, I think, in himself . . . made a lot of changes and allowed those things to happen and allowed people in the community to be responsible and so there's a whole lot less anger in the community towards him, than there [was] in the past. Because he's allowed the community to take responsibility.[23]

In addition to the systemic problems and advantages of circuit courts described above, misinterpretation of information about and of behaviour by Aboriginal offenders in the conventional justice system has been a concern.

The Misinterpretation of Aboriginal Offender Information and Behaviour at Sentencing

A further problem during sentencing of Aboriginal offenders is obtaining accurate and relevant information about the crime committed and the offender. In obtaining and assessing such information, caution must be exercised not to misinterpret interpersonal behaviours of Aboriginal offenders. Lawyer and author Rupert Ross explained the tendency of people of European descent to interpret lack of direct eye contact as indicating evasiveness, and noted that direct eye contact among the Cree and Ojibway of northwestern Ontario was a sign of disrespect as "[you] only look inferiors straight in the eye."[24]

Similarly, expectations of appropriate court behaviour may influence a judge's conclusions about the attitude of the offender. I have appeared with many Cree and Saulteaux offenders in the courts of central Saskatchewan from 1988 to the present, and I have noted that many of them respond to the stress of court by smiling or laughing nervously. This behaviour has sometimes been misinterpreted by the presiding judge as indicating a lack of respect, despite the seriousness with which the offenders viewed the proceedings when I interviewed them prior to court.

A further example of potentially misunderstood behaviour is the lack of verbal participation by Aboriginal offenders at sentencing. Such passivity may lead to an erroneous conclusion respecting offender attitude. Judge Murray Sinclair of the Provincial Court of Manitoba explained:

> A final example is the implicit expectation of lawyers, judges and juries that accused will display remorse and a desire for rehabilitation. Because their [Aboriginal offenders'] understanding of courage and their position in the overall scheme of things includes the fortitude to accept, without protest, what comes to them, Aboriginal people may react contrary to the expectations of non-Aboriginal people involved in the justice system. Many years of cultural and social oppression, combined with the high value placed on controlled emotion in the presence of strangers or authority, can result in an accused's conduct in court appearing to be inappropriate to his plea.[25]

Rupert Ross also cautioned against drawing an immediate link between lack of participation by Aboriginal offenders and lack of remorse.[26]

Language has also created problems during sentencing in Aboriginal communities. As explained by Derek Custer and Cecile Merasty of Pelican Narrows, lack of familiarity with English exacerbates fear and misunderstanding of court processes. By contrast, the Pelican Narrows sentencing circle committee, which began to meet with offenders outside of court in the spring of 1994, operated in Cree. This empowered offenders to explain their behaviour and their plan for compensating and reconciling with their victims.[27]

In Saskatchewan, problems with language at sentencing have been compounded by a shortage or absence of trained court interpreters. This has been recognized by the Saskatchewan Indian Justice Review Committee.[28] The need for a trained interpreter was clearly displayed at a sentencing circle conducted on November 14, 1994, at Pelican Narrows, Saskatchewan.[29] Of the thirty people within the circle, the only non-Cree speaking participants were the judge, a defence lawyer, two police officers, and the operator of a group home in Creighton, Saskatchewan. Approximately half of the circle's discussion was in Cree. Some comments were interpreted on an *ad hoc* basis by various circle participants, while others were left uninterpreted. Towards the conclusion of the circle, which lasted approximately two hours, Judge Fafard apologized for his poor grasp of Cree and indicated his hope that the community would soon have the benefit of a Cree-speaking judge. In contrast, a court communicator formed a regular part of the circuit court party in Manitoba. This was evidenced at court in Pukatawagan on April 11, 1995, where a court communicator was present to assist Aboriginal offenders appearing before the court.

A further difficulty with language at sentencing is incompatibility between languages. Professor Tim Quigley of the University of Saskatchewan, a former defence lawyer in northern Saskatchewan, commented on the difficulties associated with translation:

> I recall from my legal aid days being told that the Dene language does not make the same precise legal distinction between "rape" and "intercourse," something that is obviously important in a sexual assault case. Likewise, in Cree, it is apparently difficult to distinguish between an accidental pushing from an intentional one—again, a vital difference in an assault trial. Yet both languages are very precise in their own cultural contexts. It is simply that our legal system is alien and difficult to describe in those languages.[30]

My own experience with Cree people in the courts of central Saskatchewan has repeatedly evidenced their difficulty in explaining sexual interaction. Although one of the explanations of this may well be shyness and the trauma associated with the recollection of an unpleasant memory, it also appeared that the Cree language simply does not contain a similar vocabulary to English respecting sexual acts.

Aboriginal approaches to sentencing focus on greater community involvement in sentencing and more individualized sentences. What are the opportunities for increasing community participation and sentencing discretion, given the current practice in Canadian law?

4 | Opportunities for Community and Victim Participation and Sentencing Discretion in Conventional Sentencing

Canadian criminal law and procedure is governed primarily by the *Criminal Code*. Other statutes that influence Canadian sentencing law and practice, although to a lesser extent, include the *Canada Evidence Act,*[1] the *Young Offenders Act,*[2] and the *Controlled Drugs and Substances Act.*[3] Sentencing follows either a finding of guilt or a guilty plea. Most often, the sentencing hearing follows a guilty plea. The Crown counsel sets out the circumstances alleged, together with the offender's criminal record and the Crown's position on sentence. The defence counsel addresses any disputed factual areas and makes representations about the offender's personal circumstances and character, together with submissions on an appropriate sentence.

Although plenty of latitude exists for the introduction of sworn evidence that could involve the offender, the victim, or lay community members, the usual participants in the sentencing hearing are the Crown and defence lawyers and the judge. The criminal justice process, from initial complaint onwards, has an impact on a broad cross-section of community members, yet little has been done to broaden the range of participants at sentencing. Judge Barry Stuart of the Yukon Territorial Court, in *R. v. Moses,* characterized the typical sentencing hearing in Canada:

> The foreboding court-room setting discourages meaningful participation beyond lawyers and judges.
>
> The judge presiding on high, robed to emphasize his authoritative dominance, armed with the power to control the process, is rarely challenged. Lawyers by their deference, and by standing when addressing the judge, reinforce to the community the judge's pivotal importance. All of this combines to encourage the community to believe judges uniquely and exclusively possess the wisdom and resources to develop a just and viable result. They are so grievously wrong.
>
> Counsel, due to the rules, and their prominent place in the court, control the input of information. Their ease with the rules, their facility with the peculiar legal language, exudes a confidence and skill that lay people commonly perceive as a prerequisite to participate.

> The community[,] relegated to the back of the room, is separated from counsel and the judge either by an actual bar or by placing their seats at a distinct distance behind counsel tables. The interplay between lawyers and the judge creates the perception of a ritualistic play. The set, as well as the performance, discourages anyone else from participating.[4]

The *Criminal Code*, despite containing over eight hundred sections, provides limited guidance on the procedure to be followed during sentencing. Sections 723 and 724 recognize the right of both the prosecutor and the offender to present evidence and make submissions on an appropriate sentence. The judge may also require the production of evidence to be considered prior to sentencing. The offender's right to address the court prior to sentencing is recognized by section 726. Sentencing sometimes occurs after a trial; in which case the judge can form an opinion during the trial about the circumstances of the offence and the nature of the accused;[5] however, the vast majority of accused persons appearing before Canadian courts plead guilty.[6]

The Supreme Court of Canada has provided guidance respecting the range of information that may be considered during the sentencing hearing. Supreme Court Justice Ritchie, in *R.* v. *McGrath*, cited the following passage from *Crankshaw's Criminal Code of Canada,* 7th ed., with approval:

> After conviction, accurate information should be given as to the general character and other material circumstances of the prisoner *even though such information is not available in the form of evidence proper,* and such information when given can rightly be taken into consideration by the judge in determining the quantum of punishment, unless it is challenged or contradicted by or on behalf of the prisoner, in which case the judge should either direct proper proof to be given or should ignore the information.[7] [Emphasis in original]

The procedure followed during sentencing is usually less formal than that followed at trial. Although an offender may force formal proof of any disputed allegation of fact,[8] this is rare and often results in judicial substitution of a plea of not guilty. The general practice is for Crown and defence counsel to make submissions to the court on the circumstances of the offence and the offender and on appropriate sentence. The subject matter of these submissions is potentially broader than can be presented at trial. For example, a major focus at sentencing is the general character and the material circumstances of the offender, which would be largely inadmissible at trial.

In my experience as a defence lawyer practising in central Saskatchewan from 1988 to the present, I have had the opportunity of observing and participating in hundreds of sentencing hearings. In most cases, these hearings have been brief and have consisted solely of representations to the judge by Crown prosecutors (or by police officers acting for the Crown in rural court locations) and defence counsel. Sworn testimony has rarely been presented and, other than indirectly through the remarks of counsel or through comments in written pre-sentence reports, victims and local community members have rarely participated. Many factors have contributed to the simplicity and brevity of this process. The most significant among these appear to be a lack of court resources to allow for more time at sentencing and a reluctance on the part of judges, together with Crown and defence lawyers, to depart from established sentencing patterns. Clearly, the court system is faced with the challenge of finding meaningful avenues to facilitate lay participation while ensuring that offenders and victims are treated fairly.

Opportunities for Community and Victim Participation

Given that sentencing hearings are less formal than trials and given the range of information admissible at sentencing, there are a number of opportunities for victims and community members to participate in the sentencing process. Information from victims and local community members can be presented to the court through representations of counsel, often in the form of letters of support or character references. Other sources of information are court-ordered reports, including pre-sentence reports and victim-impact statements pursuant to sections 721 and 722 of the *Criminal Code* and pre-disposition reports pursuant to section 14 of the *Young Offenders Act*. Probation officers and youth workers are charged with the responsibility of preparing pre-sentence and pre-disposition reports. Sworn testimony may also be presented by defence or Crown counsel prior to sentencing.

Until recently, Crown and defence counsel and the judges have acted as gatekeepers controlling introduction of such information. Although community members and victims have a right to attend at sentencing unless excluded by the judge pursuant to section 486(1) of the *Code,* they do not have standing in the proceeding to compel presentation of their views to the judge. Recent changes to the *Code,* although codifying the range of evidence and submissions possible at sentencing, still do not compel a sentencing court to hear victim and community representations. Section 723 reads, in part:

> 723. (1) Before determining the sentence, a court shall give the prosecutor and the offender an opportunity to make submissions with respect to any facts relevant to the sentence to be imposed.

(2) The court shall hear any relevant evidence presented by the prosecutor or the offender.

(3) The court may, on its own motion, after hearing argument from the prosecutor and the offender, require the production of evidence that would assist it in determining the appropriate sentence.

By contrast, section 745.63(1)(d) of the *Code,* which forms part of the so-called faint hope clause for first-degree murderers, does require a jury to consider information provided by a victim either "at the time of the imposition of the sentence or at the time of the hearing under this section."[9] The *Young Offenders Act* requires, in section 20, that the judge consider "any pre-disposition report required by the court, any representations made by the parties to the proceedings or their counsel or agents and by the parents of the young person and any other relevant information" prior to sentencing. In addition, section 69 of this act provides for establishment of "youth justice committees" to assist in "any aspect of" the act's administration. This provision has allowed local people to become directly involved in the sentencing of young offenders. This was done in at Sandy Bay in the late 1980s. Sandy Bay resident Ina Ray explained:

> [We] were approached and asked if we would be willing to try out this new way of dealing with young offenders. I believe we were approached by the magistrate [provincial court judge] at that time, who was feeling frustrated . . . that the system wasn't working the way it was set up, in that someone from out of town, like the magistrate, would come in and, not knowing the community or the people, would deal with justice the way he believes it should be done. But he felt that it would be more effective if people from the community took responsibility and showed that they were affected and cared about the people that got into trouble. That might be a better way.[10]

The *Young Offenders Act* provides more latitude for community participation in sentencing than does the *Criminal Code.* Parents,[11] agents of the young person,[12] and members of a youth justice committee may have direct input into the sentencing of young offenders.

Given the adversarial roles usually assumed by defence and Crown counsel, the pre-sentence report has served as the court's major objective source of sentencing information. Unfortunately, the enabling section of the *Criminal Code* contains little guidance respecting the structure and content of such a report.[13] Section 721(3) of the *Code* sets limited requirements for pre-sentence reports, including the offender's age, maturity, character, attitude, willingness to make amends, criminal record, and any previous history of having been dealt with through alternate measures. An unanswered question, which has resulted in disagreement among appellate courts, is whether pre-disposition and pre-sentence reports should extend beyond simple information gathering and reporting to recommending the appropriate sentence.[14]

This is a personal concern of mine, after having read and considered a multitude of pre-sentence reports in my work as a defence lawyer. While I recognize the legitimate function of a probation officer in considering the viability of various forms of sentence, I have found a specific recommendation often serves to usurp the role of the judge, whose task is to make an independent determination. Many times such recommendations appear to become *faits accomplis*, regardless of the foundation or logic supporting them. I believe a better system would be to allow such reports to analyse all viable forms of sentence without making a specific recommendation, thereby leaving the final decision to the court after hearing sentencing representations from the Crown and the defence.

A further concern is that the *Code* does not define the term "probation officer," thereby creating uncertainty about who can author such a report. At Hollow Water First Nation, pre-sentence reports have been prepared by assessment team members of Community Holistic Circle Healing who, technically, are not probation officers employed by the Manitoba Department of Justice. This raises the question of whether the writing of pre-sentence reports can properly and lawfully be delegated by an employed probation officer.

A final problem regarding pre-sentence reports is the varying quality between reports. One author commented that "the quality of the pre-sentence report can vary enormously, depending on the time available to the probation officer, his skill, the community services assisting him, and, of course, the mode of presentation."[15] This discrepancy is troubling considering that these reports often form the primary source of information to the court about both the offender and the offence.

Although pre-sentence reports are discretionary under the *Criminal Code,* section 24(2) of the *Young Offenders Act* requires that judges consider pre-disposition reports before sentencing young offenders to custody. The act details the information required in these reports. Section 14(2) requires the report to record an interview with the young person and, if possible, with his or her parents; an interview, where possible, with the victim; the age, maturity, behaviour, and attitude of the young person; any plans of the young person; the young person's criminal record; any experience of the young person with mediation/diversion; the resources available in the community; and the school and employment records of the young person. The act allows oral submission of pre-disposition reports by youth court workers if such information cannot reasonably be committed to writing.[16]

Information about crime victims can be considered at sentencing through presentation of victim-impact statements pursuant to section 722(1) of the *Code*. Victim-impact statements include a description of "the harm done to, or loss suffered by, the victim arising from the commission of the offence." The statements are to be in writing, prepared in accordance with the procedures specifically established under a designated provincial program and shall be considered by the judge in determining an appropriate sentence. The *Criminal Code* does not require that a victim-impact statement be prepared for every sentencing.

Although only British Columbia, Alberta, New Brunswick, Nova Scotia, Prince Edward Island, and Newfoundland have designated programs, statements from victims are received in courts across all provinces and territories of Canada. Whether or not a victim-impact statement is tendered, section 722(3) of the *Code* allows the judge to consider "any other evidence concerning any victim of the offence" and opens the possibility of a court requiring testimony or the production of evidence to ascertain the effect of the offence on a victim.

Concern over lack of victim participation in the criminal justice system is not new. In the United States, the chairperson of a 1982 Presidential Task Force on Victims of Crime stated: "Somewhere along the way, the (criminal justice) system began to serve lawyers and judges and defendants, treating the victims with institutional disinterest."[17] These comments were echoed by the Canadian Federal-Provincial Task Force on Justice for Victims of Crime: "Ours is an adversarial system where the victim is not one of the adversaries."[18]

The non-mandatory nature of victim-impact statements under the Canadian *Criminal Code* stands in contrast to the evolving American procedure. The 1982 Presidential Task Force on Victims of Crime reported that more than thirty-four states and the U.S. federal legislative process required courts to consider victim-impact statements.[19] Victim-impact statements have been described as providing a voice for victims during sentencing and ensuring the court has complete information about the crime's impact upon the victim.[20] Victim's rights groups have criticized the lack of uniform usage and the discretionary nature of such statements in Canadian law. At a 1994 conference of the prominent Canadian group CAVEAT (Canadians Against Violence Everywhere Advocating its Termination), the victim's rights panel recommended "[s]tandardization and uniform use of Victim Impact Statements at all stages of the criminal justice system including sentencing."[21]

Frustration by some victims over their treatment by the justice system, including the sentencing process, has lead to the formation of various victim's rights groups. These groups lobby governments (primarily the federal government) for statutory changes and provide a public voice for concerns over the treatment of victims within the justice system. One such group, Victims of Violence, has published a Victim's Bill of Rights that includes the following provisions:

> (4.) At a victim's request, victims will be notified of and have the right to be present at all criminal proceedings . . . [including] sentencing hearings. . . .
> (6.) Victims have the right to present Victim Impact Statements, orally or written, at sentencing . . . proceedings.[22]

These groups raise a number of as-yet-unresolved questions regarding the rights of victims, including whether a victim should have a separate standing in a criminal proceeding and therefore the right to be represented by a lawyer. There is no question that such groups have become major players in the public debate over justice.

Not all victims wish to attend sentencing hearings in the presence of offenders. Nevertheless, these victims may still benefit from some direct or indirect participation in the sentencing process. Author Andrew Klein, considering a 1981 Pennsylvania study on the views of victims, commented that "the simple expedient of victim recognition, involvement, and the ordering of restitution, . . . can substantially increase victim satisfaction with the system, the sentence and the judge."[23] Similarly, Judge Stuart, in *Moses,* described the potential impact on offenders of victim participation within a sentencing circle:

> Many offenders perceive only the state as the aggrieved party. They fail to appreciate the very human pain and suffering they cause. Absent an appreciation of the victims' suffering, offenders fail to understand their sentence except as the intrusion of an insensitive, oppressive state bent on punishment. An offender's remorse is more likely to be prompted by a desire to seek mercy from the state or by a recognition that they have been "bad". Only when an offender's pain caused by the oppression of the criminal justice system is confronted by the pain that victims experience from crime, can most offenders gain a proper perspective of their behaviour. Without this perspective, the motivation to successfully pursue rehabilitation lacks an important and often essential ingredient.[24]

In addition to direct or indirect participation in sentencing in court, victims and community members may also participate in diversion of cases from the court system, referred to as "mediation/diversion" or "alternative measures."

Community and Victim Participation in Diversion Outside the Court System

Mediation/diversion programs allow offenders the opportunity to compensate and reconcile with their victims and community. Although the terms "mediation" and "diversion" are often used conjunctively, they represent two processes that only sometimes occur together. Diversion refers to the resolution of criminal acts outside the formal court system. Mediation refers to a process that involves offender and victim in an attempt to negotiate crime compensation for the victim and to achieve some measure of reconciliation between the two. Such programs are called "alternative measures" in section 717 of the *Criminal Code* and in section 4 of the *Young Offenders Act*. The *Code* diversion provisions require governmental authorization before taking effect. As of January 1998, this authorization had been granted by the federal government and by the provinces of Saskatchewan, Alberta, Nova Scotia, Prince Edward Island, and British Columbia.

In the United States, the prevalence of diversion programs for youthful offenders was shown in a study that found that "more than 50% of all delinquency cases referred to juvenile court in the U.S. . . . [were] disposed of nonjudicially (including formal and informal diversion)."[25] Similarly, "[s]ince the proclamation of the Young Offenders Act (1982), there has been a growing interest across Canada in developing opportunities for mediation and reconciliation to occur between young offenders and their victims."[26]

The philosophy of mediation/diversion can be seen in the evolution of a crime mediation program in Columbus, Ohio. This program has been described by Daniel McGillis, director of the Dispute Resolution Project at Harvard Law School:

> Some of the earliest mediation centres were developed by prosecutors frustrated by the seeming inability of the courts to effectively handle minor disputes. In 1970, the city prosecutor of Columbus, Ohio, established the Night Prosecutor Program, one of the first mediation projects in the nation. The prosecutor noticed that complainants very often withdrew their complaints as trial time drew near because their opponents were neighbours, relatives, or acquaintances. The complainants rarely sought jail terms or fines for their adversaries, but rather were looking for an apology, changed behaviour, or money paid to them as restitution. . . . Now more than 10,000 matters a year are mediated in Columbus.[27]

Clearly, a motivating factor behind the development of mediation programs has been the opportunity for victims to seek redress from and resolution with offenders away from the often confrontational and impersonal courtroom.

The process of mediation involves what has come to be called "restorative justice." Restorative justice allows the offender to acknowledge the harm done to the victim and provides an opportunity to repair, to the extent possible, the relationship between the parties. The necessity of local community resources and support cannot be overstated when considering this approach. In *Taylor,*[28] Chief Justice Bayda of the Saskatchewan Court of Appeal commented that "without a community willing to help to restore and re-integrate the offender into the community the restorative approach is doomed to fail."

Restorative justice is most often associated with rural and isolated areas, where the close-knit nature of communities necessitates a restoration of harmony between offender, victim, and community following a transgression. However, two urban mediation/diversion programs in Toronto have demonstrated that this approach can also be applied in a large urban setting. The community sentencing model of Operation Springboard[29] was based on the circle sentencing experience of Canadian Aboriginal communities. It administered mediation/diversion programs for both young offenders and young adults in Canada's largest city. The community council project of the Aboriginal Legal Services of Toronto[30] applied the young offender mediation/diversion concept to adult Aboriginal offenders. This project used the model of a community or elders' council drawn from Toronto's Aboriginal community to fashion appropriate dispositions for offenders while, at the same time, promoting reconciliation and healing.

Despite the support for restorative justice in Aboriginal communities, many factors originating both within and outside of a specific community affect the availability of alternative forms and severities of sentence. Among these influential "outside" factors are decisions on sentencing from appellate courts.

The Role of Appellate Review in Sentencing Discretion

The *Criminal Code* provides broad sentencing discretion.[31] For example, penalties for the offence of assault causing bodily harm[32] range from an absolute discharge to ten years in prison. In theory, this discretion may be used in adapting sentences to the circumstances of individual offenders. Former Supreme Court Justice Emmett Hall advocated an individualized approach to sentencing:

> Some judges have adopted the policy of treating all offenders convicted of similar or identical offences alike. This is a practice which should not be condoned. It is the offender, not the offence which should dictate what penalty should be imposed in the circumstances. The court should stand firm in

dealing humanely with wrongdoers—young or old; native or alien; white or coloured; all as individuals. Revenge or retribution are no part of a court's function. We can and are entitled to have law and order but not at the expense of justice to the individual.[33]

Yet, in reality, sentencing discretion is often limited. Although many factors potentially enter into a sentencing decision,[34] appellate court guidelines (which establish acceptable ranges of sentence and in some cases "starting points" for specific offences) act to significantly restrict discretion and hence the use of innovative approaches to sentencing.

The effect of appellate review on sentencing practice has been explained by Professor Tim Quigley of the University of Saskatchewan:

[I]n the law of sentencing, provincial courts of appeal act as both the final appellate body on the quantum of sentence and the policy-making body. Courts of appeal established starting point sentences for particular offences as a guideline to trial judges. Because of the doctrine of *stare decisis,* those guidelines become mandatory guidelines in the sense that a trial judge can only deviate from the starting point according to the presence of aggravating or mitigating factors. Otherwise, the sentence is very likely to be overturned on appeal on the ground of unexplained disparity with the sentences normally imposed in that jurisdiction for that offence. This policy is deeply entrenched in the Saskatchewan Court of Appeal. This policy is a major constraint on innovation and creativity by trial judges.[35]

In Manitoba, the AJI commissioners recognized what they termed to be "a disturbing aspect of appellate sentencing," which was "the tendency of appellate courts simply to impose their own sentence in place of that of the lower court, instead of reviewing the lower court decision to ensure that it complies with principles of sound sentencing practices."[36] The Supreme Court of Canada has recently commented on the approach to be applied by appellate courts when considering sentence appeals. In a series of judgements,[37] this court appears to have approved a strong deference to the sentencing decision taken by a trial judge. In *R.* v. *Shropshire,* Justice Iacobucci of the Supreme Court of Canada stated:

An appellate court should not be given free rein to modify a sentencing order simply because it feels that a different order ought to have been made. The formulation of a sentencing order is a profoundly subjective process; the trial Judge has the advantage of having seen and heard all of the witnesses whereas the appellate Court can only base itself upon a written record. A variation in the sentence should only be made if the Court of Appeal is convinced it is not fit. That is to say, that it has found the sentence to be clearly unreasonable.[38]

In *R.* v. *M.(C.A.),* Chief Justice Lamer of the Supreme Court of Canada stated:

> Put simply, absence an error in principle, failure to consider a relevant factor, or an overemphasis of the appropriate factors, a court of appeal should only intervene to vary a sentence imposed at trial if the sentence is demonstrably unfit. Parliament explicitly vested sentencing judges with a discretion to determine the appropriate degree and kind of punishment under the *Criminal Code.*[39]

In *R.* v. *Horvath,*[40] Chief Justice Bayda of the Saskatchewan Court of Appeal, speaking for a unanimous court, commented on the effect of these decisions:

> The strong deferential approach enunciated in *Shropshire, M.(C.A.)* and *McDonnell* differs from and must now be substituted for the much lower deferential approach heretofore used by this court as exemplified by such cases as *R.* v. *Morrissette* . . . , *R.* v. *Wenarchuck* (1982), 67 C.C.C. (2d) 169, *R.* v. *Dunn* (1995), 95 C.C.C. (3d) 289, *R.* v. *Manjanatha,* [1995] 8 W.W.R. 101 and *R.* v. *Morin* (1995), 101 C.C.C. (3d) 124.[41]

It will be interesting to observe whether this change in the standard of appellate review translates into the application of greater discretion by lower court judges and hence less adherence to previously observed appellate sentencing ranges and starting-point sentences. This will be especially significant for counsel practising in rural or northern areas or in Aboriginal communities.

Despite the goal of sentence parity, there is no question that regional differences in sentences occur. Statistics released by the Saskatchewan Department of Justice indicated that between September 1, 1996, and March 31, 1997, 67 percent of the conditional sentences granted in Saskatchewan had occurred in the Prince Albert, North Battleford, and northern regions (an area with a relatively small proportion of the Saskatchewan's population). It is to be hoped that the Supreme Court decisions cited above will allow more flexibility at the local level. This would permit sentences consistent with the wishes of local community members, including those victimized by the offender's actions, even though they may be inconsistent with ranges established by appellate courts. Indeed, Chief Justice Lamer in *M.(C.A.)* recognized the unique position of the sentencing judge in relation to the local community:

A sentencing judge also possesses the unique qualifications of experience and judgment from having served on the front lines of our criminal justice system. Perhaps most importantly, the sentencing judge will normally preside near or within the community which has suffered the consequences of the offender's crime. As such, the sentencing judge will have a strong sense of the particular blend of sentencing goals that will be "just and appropriate" for the protection of that community.[42]

A related and ongoing issue is what standards and values should be applied in determining the best interests of a community. Should these be, as almost always argued by the Crown, the standards and values of the broader provincewide or nationwide community, or should these be the values, standards, and, indeed, aspirations of the local community? The above passage from the Supreme Court appears to place greater weight on local considerations.

Appellate review may have a considerable effect on judicial innovation and creativity in sentencing, as evidenced by the majority decision of the Northwest Territories Court of Appeal in *R*. v. *Naqitarvik*.[43] In the lower court, Judge Bourassa of the Territorial Court of the Northwest Territories was persuaded by community representations made about traditional Inuit treatment of offenders; he sentenced the offender to ninety days intermittent incarceration and probation on a sexual assault charge, a sentence unquestionably outside the appellate range for this offence. In increasing the offender's original sentence to eighteen months' incarceration, Justice Laycraft of the Northwest Territories Court of Appeal stressed adherence to accepted appellate guidelines:

> I follow *Sandercock*[44] in using a sentence of imprisonment of three years as a starting point in cases of major sexual assault. No doubt some of the aggravating and mitigating factors mentioned in that case may be somewhat modified when applied to northern Canada. . . . Nevertheless, *Sandercock* offers a general guide-line of the starting point and of the various factors involved in upward or downward revision of that starting point in the light of aggravating or mitigating factors. . . . [O]n a consideration of all of the factors of this case, I find the sentence to be wholly inadequate.[45]

As community-based sentences have flexibility and can be adapted to local circumstances, appellate guidelines that require significant periods of incarceration for specific offences, such as sexual assault, act as a deterrent to innovative sentences. Of the specific initiatives studied in this book, only the Community Holistic Circle Healing project (CHCH) at Hollow Water regularly considered sexual offences. In Saskatchewan, Judge Fafard acknowledged his hesitancy in dealing with cases of sexual assault by way of a sentencing circle:

> If you get a community [that] develops a kind of a Hollow Water model, to do for instance, sexual assault cases, then we'll be able to venture out into that field, because people would like to do those. [However], we just feel we don't have the resources at the local level [to do such cases] . . . but right now I don't think we're really . . . equipped to do those kind of cases in a sentencing circle.[46]

Judge Fafard's comments also raise the value, if not the necessity, of local treatment and support resources to support sentences that provide an alternative to jail.

The importance of these resources was seen recently at Stanley Mission, Saskatchewan. The Stanley Mission Justice Committee had begun to use traditional holistic practices in dealing with alcoholism and youth suicide. Two sexual assault cases were referred to this committee by the Provincial Court in La Ronge, apparently to allow the offenders to participate in holistic treatment similar to that being practised through CHCH at Hollow Water. After allegations that one offender had approached his victim at her school contrary to his court order, the Lac La Ronge Indian band disbanded the committee, claiming that it was not yet ready for the serious cases undertaken.[47] Members of the disbanded committee, however, claimed the band's action represented discrimination against "traditional Native healing in favour of Christianity."[48] The Provincial Court, in sentencing both offenders charged with sexual assault, found the band's actions constituted political interference in the court's process. Both offenders were sentenced to conditional sentences of imprisonment. The Saskatchewan Court of Appeal reversed both sentences and imposed penitentiary terms.[49]

Despite the limiting effects of appellate guidelines, many sentences rendered in northern Saskatchewan still appear to be inconsistent with accepted appellate ranges for given offences. As an example, the Pelican Narrows circle produced sentences that likely fall outside the range of sentences accepted by the Saskatchewan Court of Appeal. All ten offenders dealt with in that circle were charged with aggravated assault (carrying a maximum penalty of fourteen years' imprisonment for an adult or two years' closed custody for a young offender). This incident was serious as the victim had been dragged from his home by the offenders, who had proceeded to beat and kick him repeatedly leaving him unconscious and bloodied. The police could not wake the victim initially and sought medical attention for him, which indicated possible seizures and a swelling of the brain. The sentencing circle reached a consensus that nine of the offenders (none of whom had previous records) should either receive suspended sentences including probation or simply probation (depending on whether the offender was a young offender or an adult). One offender with a previous record was given four months' open custody followed by probation. This consensus was supported by the Crown, represented by the RCMP. The discrepancy between these sentences and existing appellate ranges, and the lack of appeal by the Crown, is likely explained by support for such sentences by Crown representatives (in this case, the police) at the circle.

The importance of Crown support for innovative sentencing approaches cannot be overstated. In Manitoba, Crown support at two sentencing circles at Hollow Water was crucial as both cases involved serious sexual assaults on children that would normally have drawn significant penitentiary terms. However, in both cases, the Crown attorney joined the circle consensus for a suspended sentence with a probation order focussed on holistic sexual offender treatment at Hollow Water. Neither case was appealed.

In addressing the over-representation of Aboriginal people in Canadian jails, Professor Tim Quigley advocated a legislative or judicial affirmative action program providing lower sentences for Aboriginal persons:

> Undoubtedly, the notion of affirmative action in sentencing will be controversial. I suspect the idea that all offenders committing the same offence should receive the same or nearly the same penalty is deeply ingrained. The law and order mentality that commands us to get tough with crime also leads us in the opposite direction from healing and reintegration. But if we are serious about dealing with our social ills, if we are serious about our commitment to justice for Aboriginal people, and if we are serious about true equality, we should accept the concept of special measures for Aboriginal offenders. After all, the larger society must bear a large portion of the responsibility for the plight in which Aboriginal people find themselves. . . . It would be desirable, of course, if the political will were there to have such a scheme implemented by legislation. But that may not occur. As an alternative, it is open to the Canadian judiciary to develop such a plan. . . . *Given that provincial courts of appeal are in general the court of last resort on quantum of sentence and are also in a better position to appreciate the situation within their own provinces, it would be logical for that level of court to devise and supervise such a program.*[50] [Emphasis added]

Although judicial affirmative action could be achieved through the broad sentencing discretion given to judges by the *Criminal Code,* appellate authority intent on upholding the principle of sentence uniformity reduces the likelihood that judges would regularly impose sentences outside provincial appellate ranges. Despite the apparent leniency of many sentences passed at the court I attended at Sandy Bay on April 19, 1995, Judge Fafard noted to one offender that he could not accede to the offender's request for a community-based sentence for a violent crime as he "had to pass these sentences through the Court of Appeal."[51]

Once again, Crown support of new sentencing approaches is highly significant. Judge Robert Kopstein of the Provincial Court of Manitoba, who was involved in an elders' sentencing panel at the Rousseau River Reserve in the late 1970s, acknowledged the futility of attempting new sentencing approaches without Crown support.[52] Closely intermeshed with the issue of Crown support is whether the positions taken by the Crown reflect the views and aspirations of local Aboriginal communities or whether they reflect only the views of society as a whole.

Insight into the interplay between local community input in sentencing and other factors, such as appellate court authority, can be found south of our border. In the United States, the final decision on sentence is, in many cases, left to members of the jury rather than to the judge.

Jury Sentencing in the United States

The United States shares with Canada a criminal law system that originated in England. Despite this common heritage, the sentencing process currently existing in several American states differs markedly from prevailing practice in both England and Canada. Most American states sanctioning capital punishment leave death penalty decisions to the jury.[53] Eight states allow juries hearing non-capital cases to sentence offenders.[54]

The American experience stands in sharp contrast to the limited sentencing role of juries in Canada. In Canada, the only provisions allowing jury participation in sentencing are section 745.2 of the *Criminal Code*, which allows a jury to recommend the number of years to parole for a convicted second-degree murderer, and section 745.63, which empowers a jury to decide whether the time before an inmate, serving life after having been sentenced to parole eligibility of more than fifteen years, can apply for parole should be reduced. However, the actual, as opposed to theoretical, power of juries in Canada is now debatable after the actions of the second trial jury in *Latimer*.[55] The jury in that case recommended that Robert Latimer be eligible for parole after only one year of his sentence. This recommendation appears to have been given significant weight by the judge in arriving at his decision on sentence.

Reasons suggested for community involvement in sentencing in the United States include mistrust of Crown-appointed judges in colonial courts[56] and the historical prevalence of lay judges, which leads to the conclusion that there is little difference between judge and jury in terms of experience, training, and competence.[57]

As jury sentencing represents the ultimate extension of community sentencing participation, what has been its impact? The National Advisory Committee on Criminal Justice Standards has criticized jury sentencing in non-capital cases:

> [T]he practice has been condemned by every serious study and analysis in the last half century. Jury sentencing is non-professional and is more likely than judge sentencing of being arbitrary and based on emotions rather than the needs of the offender or society. Sentencing by juries leads to disparate sentences and leaves little opportunity for development of sentencing policies.[58]

Objections to jury sentencing in non-capital cases include the greater disparity in sentences between like cases;[59] lack of information respecting offenders possessed by juries in comparison with judges, who could adjourn sentencing for a pre-sentence report;[60] the tendency of jury sentences to represent a compromise or average of the various opinions of jurors (many of which may be totally unreasonable and/or irrational);[61] lack of juror sentencing experience;[62] and the tendency of jurors to be swayed by emotion and prejudice.[63] Arguments in favour of jury sentencing have been summarized by Judge Charles Betts of the 98th District Court in Texas:

1. The anonymity of jurors makes them less subject to the pressures of public feelings and opinion than the elected judge, who must seek popular favour at the next election.
2. The brief tenure of the jury makes corruption or improper influence especially difficult.
3. Jury-fixed punishment diminishes popular mistrust of official justice.
4. The judgement of the jury may be more sensitive than that of the judge because its members, unlike the judge, are not often confronted with the recurrent problems of court cases and therefore do not become calloused.
5. A jury lacking sentencing power tends to acquit a defendant it believes guilty when it fears that the sentence the judge will impose is probably too severe.
6. Because it is a composite, a jury levels individual opinions and provides a reconciliation of varied temperaments, and therefore is more apt to assess a fair punishment.[64]

Despite the limited role given to jurors in Canada under the *Criminal Code,* circle sentencing may, to some extent, be considered a parallel to jury sentencing, as these circles involve lay participants in the process of seeking a consensus on appropriate sentence. This approach was described by Judge Stuart in *Moses:*

> The circle, by engaging everyone in the discussion, engaged everyone in the responsibility of finding an answer. The final sentence evolved from the input of everyone in the circle. The consensus-based approach fostered not just shared responsibility, but instilled a shared concern to ensure the sentence was successfully implemented.[65]

Although some similarities may be drawn between American sentencing juries and community sentencing approaches in Canada, the American experience remains an interesting contrast. One obvious difference between approaches is that sentencing circle participants are often present because of their closeness to the offender or victim. Jury members, on the other hand, although representing the community at large, are excluded from participation if acquainted with offender or victim. Both approaches, however, depend upon the participation of local non-professional community members in a process otherwise dominated by professionals.

Canadian criminal law allows broad discretion respecting both the process and practice of sentencing and the actual sentence imposed. It is clear, however, that limits are placed on offender, victim, and local community participation at sentencing within conventional Canadian court practice. The obvious question is what new approaches are available to change conventional process and practice.

A Search for New Approaches

In the conventional Canadian justice system, Crown prosecutors represent both victims and community members at sentencing.[66] Although evidence of their views is tendered by defence or Crown counsel, community members and victims are not considered parties to the sentencing hearing. Comments by Justice de Weerdt of the Northwest Territories Supreme Court in *R.* v. *Cabot-Blanc* reflect the prominence of defence and Crown counsel within the conventional sentencing hearing:

> As to the task force recommendations [the Task Force on Spousal Assault in the Northwest Territories, 1985] . . . to the effect that the courts should spend more time on the spousal assault cases and find ways to have the evidence of community action groups and leaders placed before the courts (at the same time urging community initiatives such as informing the judiciary of "community attitudes and expectations regarding the crime of spousal assault and

its punishment"), *I think that it should be said here that it is the function of counsel to ensure that pertinent evidence is adduced before the courts, and that it is not appropriate for courts to turn themselves into inquisitors, investigators or commissions of inquiry in that connection.*[67] [Emphasis added]

Several Canadian inquiries into the treatment of Aboriginal people within the Canadian justice system have questioned the lack of direct community input at sentencing. The AJI in Manitoba commented:

> If non-Aboriginal judges and courts are going to be able to formulate sentences which are appropriate to the needs of Aboriginal offenders, victims and communities, they will need direct input from those communities. . . . In particular, communities need to be involved in the sentencing process, since sentences should, in part, reflect the needs and desires of the community.[68]

The Saskatchewan Indian Justice Review Committee reached a similar conclusion:

> In order to empower aboriginal communities and reduce feeling of alienation, communities must be given an opportunity to become involved in, and take greater responsibility in community interaction with, the criminal justice system. . . . Changes in sentencing or remand practices to recognize community-based approaches cannot succeed without the full participation and support of the judiciary at all levels and of Crown counsel.[69]

Support for direct consultation with the community has also come from the judiciary. Chief Judge Lilles of the Yukon Territorial Court stated in *R. v. J.A.P.:*

> There are many benefits to be gained from citizen and community participation in sentencing and dispositions. Such participation reinforces the socializing effect of the criminal law upon many persons in the community. It strengthens the community focus tending to reduce crime and enhance[s] community interest in the administration of justice. The educative impact of community dispositions cannot be overstated.[70]

Judge Stuart, of the same court, echoed these sentiments in commenting that "the formal, professional justice system must acquire greater confidence and trust in community knowledge, judgement and instincts."[71]

Fieldwork I conducted in Saskatchewan and Manitoba disclosed significant local interest in community participation at sentencing on the basis of intimate knowledge of the victim and offender. Donald McKay, Jr., a Cree from Cumberland House, explained:

Well, one of the biggest things I believe in with the sentencing circle is the community knows the person that has committed whatever kind of crime or whatever it was. We . . . know the accused and we know the victim. We know him I think far more than the court system, the judge, or the lawyers . . . probation officers or social services [employees] that come in. We know him more than anybody else. I think we can better deal with these people.[72]

Feelings of estrangement from non-resident judges and probation officers were voiced, together with cries for local participation. Greg Bragstad, a Sandy Bay resident and sentencing circle participant, commented:

[T]he judge flies in from La Ronge. He's here at 8:00 [a.m.] and he's gone [later that day]. The community members are saying: we don't want this kind of [offender] action in our community, so it puts more onus on the person than the judge saying it.[73]

Local sentencing and mediation participation was seen as a means of community empowerment. When asked if the sentencing circle committee was going to make a difference in Cumberland House, chairperson Cyril Roy commented:

Well, that's what I'm hoping for and I'm sure I'm not the only person hoping for that. At least that might help our community and looking at these people coming to the sentencing circle [committee], they respond to the people that are in that circle, and I'm sure that . . . in the future there's more people . . . being involved in the circle. Because that's the only way we can keep our community a little stronger and keep it going.[74]

Given this clear interest in enhancing community participation, how might it be facilitated?

A number of community sentencing approaches have been employed in Aboriginal communities across Canada. In September 1994 a workshop on the role of Crown counsel in Aboriginal contexts was held in Vancouver. Prosecutors from across Canada[75] reported on community sentencing initiatives within their jurisdictions.[76] Although the draft report represented only a summary of the personal experiences of prosecutors from some of Canada's provincial and territorial jurisdictions, these comments served as a guide to the range of sentencing approaches being used within Aboriginal communities. The report showed that circle sentencing was being used extensively in the Yukon and to a lesser extent in Quebec, Manitoba, and Saskatchewan. Involving local elders or other community representatives in advising judges on sentencing was common in the Yukon and the Northwest Territories. A community-based model of mediation/diversion was said to be developing in Saskatchewan and Alberta.

In the six communities in this study, several community sentencing and mediation projects are described. Sandy Bay was the first community in Saskatchewan to use formal sentencing circles, commencing in the summer of 1992. A committee was also formed to make sentencing recommendations on cases referred to it by the court. At Pelican Narrows the first sentencing circle was held in the spring of 1994. A sentencing circle committee had been formed on the initiative of the local band. A number of cases were referred to this committee, which went on to conduct a sentencing circle in Cree and without a judge; this circle then presented sentencing recommendations to the court. At Cumberland House, the Provincial Court introduced circle sentencing; the sentencing circle committee functioned both as a sentence advisory committee, providing the court with community recommendations on sentencing for cases referred by the court, and as a mediation committee, dealing with adult and young offender cases referred to it by the RCMP or the court.

In Manitoba, the Hollow Water Community Holistic Circle Healing (CHCH) provided holistic treatment for sexual assault victims and victimizers. This process intersected with the Provincial Court system, initially through CHCH assessment team members providing sentencing reports to the court sitting in Pine Falls, and then, aided by a protocol with the provincial Department of Justice, through the introduction of circle sentencing at Hollow Water in 1993. An elders' advisory panel was introduced in Waywayseecappo in 1994, with local elders sitting beside the presiding judge and advising on sentences. At Pukatawagan, the local justice committee mediated cases referred to it by the RCMP, the court, and local community members; the committee also sat with the presiding judge in court and advised on sentences.

The next part of this book deals with several approaches that provide alternatives to conventional sentencing practice. These approaches are described and discussed through case studies of the Aboriginal communities mentioned above.

2 | Case Studies

5 | The Sentencing Circle

The decision in *Moses*[1] articulated concerns about conventional sentencing practices in Canadian Aboriginal communities and presented a new approach for sentencing called a sentencing circle. This is a sentencing hearing conducted in circle format. It usually involves the judge, defence and Crown counsel, police, the offender, the victim, the probation officer, and assorted community members. These participants confer in an attempt to agree on an appropriate sentence for the offender. The evolving process through which a number of sentencing circles have been conducted in specific communities is referred to as circle sentencing. In introducing this new process, Judge Stuart of the Yukon stated:

> For centuries, the basic organization of the court has not changed. Nothing has been done to encourage meaningful participation by the accused, the victim or by the community. . . . If the objective of the sentencing process is now to enhance sentencing options, to afford greater concern to the impact on victims, to shift focus from punishment to rehabilitation, and to meaningfully engage communities in sharing responsibility for sentencing decisions, it may be advantageous for the justice system to consider how court procedures and the physical arrangements within court-rooms militate against these new objectives.[2]

The conventional sentencing hearing, repeated thousands of times a day across Canada, involves interaction between defence and Crown counsel and the judge. These participants, located in the front portion of the court, are separated from lay members of the community physically (often by a bar dividing the courtroom) and symbolically by their manner of dress and their familiarity with legal process and language. By contrast, Judge Stuart, described the physical setting of the sentencing circle in *Moses:*

> For court, a circle to seat 30 people was arranged as tightly as numbers allowed. When all seats were occupied, additional seating was provided in an outer circle for persons arriving after the "hearing" had commenced.
>
> Defence sat beside the accused and his family. The Crown sat immediately across the circle from defence counsel to the right of the judge. Officials and members from the First Nation, the RCMP officers, the probation officer and others were left to find their own comfortable place in the circle.[3]

Although the physical setting of circles varied between judges, communities, and jurisdictions, there was commonality between the circles considered in this study. All involved the offender, the judge, a Crown representative, and a number of influential and respected local community members. Other participants were usually the victim, defence counsel, and family members of the offender and victim. Most of the circles had between twenty and thirty participants.

The circle setting has promoted a sense of informality and equality among participants. Judge Stuart described the egalitarian effect of the circle setting on participants:

> The circle significantly breaks down the dominance that traditional court-rooms accord the lawyers and judges. In a circle, the ability to contribute, the importance and credibility of any input is not defined by seating arrangements. The audience is changed. All persons within the circle must be addressed. Equally, anyone in the circle may ask a direct question to anyone else.[4]

During a Saskatchewan sentencing circle I attended at the Kinistin Reserve Community Hall in September 1993, participants drank coffee, smoked, and kept their hats on, all practices forbidden in conventional court.[5] This informality facilitated an interchange of opinions and information within the circle.

This sense of equality, however, may be hindered by changing the physical setting. A sentencing circle conducted in Winnipeg on January 9, 1995,[6] provided an interesting insight. Initially the chairs had been set in a circle with no other furniture in place. Shortly before the commencement of the circle, apparently at the request of the judge, a table was moved in front of the chair designated for the judge. Some in attendance commented on the effect of the special arrangements for the judge. Indeed the added table gave the impression of setting the judge apart from the rest of the circle. Although one of the reasons for the table might have been to allow the judge to make notes, this difference in treatment was noticed by those in attendance.

Robin Ritter of La Ronge,[7] one of the first defence lawyers in Saskatchewan to be involved in circle sentencing, described the practice of circle sentencing in northern Saskatchewan:

> The people take their places in the circle and the judge, or the person organizing the circle, will usually ask one of the elders to say a prayer or to perform the sacred Sweet Grass Ceremony. All religious beliefs are tolerated and welcomed. Everyone in the circle has the chance to talk or to remain silent. The members of the circle discuss the offender and his crime until they all agree on what his sentence should be. The judge then imposes that sentence according to law.[8]

Sue Davies, a probation officer with extensive involvement in circle sentencing, summarized the practice in the Yukon:

> The basic process for a "circle court" is the same from community to community. . . . The judge acts more as a chairperson or mediator in some cases, and sits in the circle with everyone else. . . . Initially, the judge or a member of the support group will welcome people to the circle court and introductions are made around the circle to assist the court recorder and familiarize people with those present. The Crown will present the circumstances of the offence, the community perception of the seriousness of the crime and make submissions as to sentence. . . . The members of the circle are asked by the judge to consider the problem and possible solutions. This allows the community to become specific when talking about the needs, strengths and resources available for the individual [offender] before them. The accused will be asked to address the circle and often speaks with much emotion and insight into their situation. If the victim is present, they are asked to speak to the circle.[9]

The focus of the circle sentencing evolving in Saskatchewan and the Yukon appears to be achieving consensus among participants. This consensus-building approach differs from the approach used by presiding judges at Pukatawagan, Manitoba. According to lawyer Joyce Dalmyn,[10] the practice of the Manitoba judges was to listen to sentence recommendations from circle participants and then to indicate their decision. These judges took a less active role in facilitating the circle and seeking consensus. Such differences suggest that the influence of local circumstances on the development of circle sentencing has led to unique practices in each community. Indeed, judicial flexibility and accommodation to local customs and practices have proved to be crucial in the development of circle sentencing within specific communities. The importance of these qualities was reflected in the comments of Judge Stuart:

> I am reluctant to set out the procedures, guidelines, the mechanics of Circle Sentencing. Reluctant to do so because there is no single model. Each community adapts Circle Sentencing to fit their particular circumstances. A principal value of Circle Sentencing lies in its flexibility to bend to the vision of each community.[11]

Chief Justice Bayda, in his dissenting judgement in *Morin*,[12] also warned that the sentencing judge "should be sensitive to the cultural tenets and customs of the community in question" and should "make whatever accommodations are necessary, within reason, to make the circle as effective as it possibly can be."[13]

The unique position of the sentencing judge in relation to the local community has recently been recognized by Chief Justice Lamer of the Supreme Court of Canada in *M.(C.A.)*.[14] This unique position may, to some degree, explain the variety of justice practices and initiatives that have developed in individual communities, and the types and levels of sentences that have resulted in individual cases. Many sentences rendered within the community justice initiatives studied in this book may appear inconsistent with the sentences being imposed elsewhere in the province and country. These sentences, however, may, at the same time, be completely consistent with the wishes and aspirations of local community members and the victim.

The Pelican Narrows circle provided an interesting insight into the evolving process of circle sentencing in northern Saskatchewan. This circle involved ten offenders, both adults and youths, charged with a serious assault on a youth. This circle had twenty-five participants, including Judge Fafard, the offenders, members of their families and other community members, two police officers, and a defence counsel. The victim was not in attendance as Judge Fafard had recently sentenced him to custody in another case. The circle opened with a prayer in Cree by a local elder. Judge Fafard outlined the range of sentence under the *Criminal Code* and the *Young Offenders Act* for the offences involved. All offenders were charged with aggravated assault, which carries a maximum penalty under the *Criminal Code* of fourteen years' imprisonment and under the *Young Offenders Act* of two years' closed custody. Corporal Bob MacMillan outlined the circumstances of the offence. The offenders had forced their way into the victim's home, where they had kicked and beaten him. The police believed beer bottles and logs had been used in the beating, which left the victim unconscious and bleeding.

Circle participants took turns speaking to the offenders and suggesting appropriate sentences. A consensus developed that one offender, the only one with a previous record and apparently the instigator of the assault, should not receive the same sentence as the other nine because he had already appeared before the committee on a similar charge. Circle participants felt he should receive a short jail sentence, followed by probation with conditions similar to those imposed on the other nine offenders. These conditions included attending counselling sessions at the local alcohol rehabilitation centre, undertaking 156 hours of community service work, abstaining from the possession or use of alcohol or firearms, taking an anger management course, and writing an apology to the victim. These conditions had been drawn up by the sentencing circle committee, who had met during the week prior to court to consider these cases.

Much interest has been expressed over the physical changes to court procedure brought about by circle sentencing. Less attention has been focussed on the legal status and effect of recommendations produced by sentencing circle participants. This is discussed in detail in the following section.

Status of Circle Recommendations in the Criminal Code

Judicial analysis of the role of circle sentencing has been varied. In *R.* v. *Rich (S.) (No. 1)*,[15] Justice O'Regan of Newfoundland's Supreme Court (Trial Division) viewed its role within the existing system as "a form of diversion in the sentencing process" whose function was to "strongly suggest alternatives to incarceration."[16] Judge Desjardins of the New Brunswick Provincial Court described the sentencing circle in *R.* v. *Nicholas* as "embracing the trappings of a conventional sentencing hearing and the sacred teaching of the native way of life" and commented that this process was "a small but tangible beginning of a bridge across the cultural divide."[17] In *Taylor,* Justice Milliken of Saskatchewan's Court of Queen's Bench likened a sentencing circle to a pre-sentence report and stated that "[t]he only difference appears . . . to be that a pre-sentence report is prepared by a probation office in writing." He pointed out that "[t]he same persons who are at a circle are usually interviewed for a pre-sentence report."[18] On appeal, Chief Justice Bayda viewed a much broader role for circle sentencing:

> A sentencing circle is much more than a fact-finding exercise with an aboriginal twist. While it may and does serve as a tool in assisting the judge to fashion a "fit" sentence, and in that respect serves much the same purpose as a pre-sentence report, a sentencing circle transcends that purpose. It is a stock-taking and accountability exercise not only on the part of the offender but on the part of the community that produced the offender. The exercise is conducted on a quintessentially human level with all interested parties in juxtaposition speaking face to face, informally, with little or no regard to legal status, as opposed to a clinical, formal level where only those parties with legal status participate and only at their respective traditional physical, cultural and ceremonial distances from each other. The exercise permits not only a release of information but a purging of feelings, a paving of the way for new growth, and a reconciliation between the offender and those he or she has hurt. The community to which the offender has accounted assumes an authority over and responsibility for the offender—an authority normally entrusted to professional public officials to whom the offender does not feel accountable.[19]

In *Moses,*[20] Judge Stuart described the role of circle sentencing as enhancing sentencing options, affording greater concern for victims, shifting the focus from punishment to rehabilitation, and meaningfully engaging communities in shared responsibility for sentencing decisions.

Despite these general comments on the role and advantages of circle sentencing, there has been little judicial consideration of the legal impact and significance of sentencing circle recommendations within the sentencing framework of the *Criminal Code*. Judge Dutil of the Court of Quebec (Criminal and Penal Division),[21] when interviewed by *Maclean's* magazine, viewed circle sentencing as an adapted sentencing hearing within the *Criminal Code* system:

> "This is an experiment," [said] Dutil. "It's a way to help me make sentences much like I use pre-sentencing reports prepared by probation officers." As such, the use of sentencing circles did not require any legislative change. "A judge can use any normal and legal means to find acceptable sentences," he [said].[22]

Available judicial comment suggests circle sentencing is based in the court's broad sentencing discretion, which retains for the judge ultimate decision-making power. Justice Sherstobitoff of the Saskatchewan Court of Appeal stated in *Morin:*

> Since there is no provision in the *Criminal Code* for the use of sentencing circles, it is implicit in their use . . . that when sentencing circles are used, the power and duty to impose a fit sentence remains vested exclusively in the trial judge. If a sentencing circle is used, and it recommends a sentence which is not a fit sentence, the judge is duty bound to ignore the recommendation to the extent that it varies from what is a fit sentence.[23]

An interesting comment on the question of which person or body controls the sentencing decision can be found in *R.* v. *John*. Justice Cote of the Alberta Court of Appeal stressed the effect of appellate sentencing guidelines both on a judge and on a sentencing circle:

> What binds a sentencing judge binds him or her with or without such community involvement. We think that if one wants to regard the sentencing circle or some similar body as being the sentencing body, it also is bound.[24]

It is not clear whether the court meant to raise the possibility of decision-making power by a sentencing circle as a whole or simply was unaware of the process followed.

Despite the judge's ultimate sentencing discretion, a prominent goal of circle sentencing is to promote both community involvement in conducting the circle and consensus among participants during the circle. The interplay between community involvement and decision making on the one hand and judicial sentencing discretion on the other was described by Judge Desjardins in *Nicholas:*

> It is very important that the judge be willing not only to convene the circle but to allow the development of the circle to originate primarily from the community. He or she must be prepared to relinquish his or her mantle of power and control with only one exception: the ultimate decision, and he or she should be prepared to adopt the decision of the circle so long as it falls within the scope of a fit and proper sentence. If I had retained control of who participated and the form of the process, the community participation would have been perfunctory.[25]

Given the judge's ultimate sentencing power, it is reasonable to expect that confusion might arise among circle participants who are asked to shape an offender's sentence yet who do not have final authority to impose it. Justice Co-ordinator Mary Crnkovich reported such confusion at the sentencing circle in *R. v. Naappaluk:*[26]

> Judge Dutil attempted to clarify what his role and the roles of the other participants would be. He explained that everyone in the circle was "on the same level" and "equal". There was no doubt some confusion was caused when after stressing this equality, he explained that he was "not obliged to follow advice" given by the circle members. . . .
> The idea of the circle is to "break down the dominance that traditional court rooms accord lawyers and judges". Referring to the group's work as "advice" while stressing the equality of everyone in the circle presents a mixed message and questions how "equal" the members really were.[27]

More experience with and exposure to court processes may help to alleviate confusion on the part of lay participants; however, the reality of conventional criminal law in Canada is that the final sentencing decision rests with the judge.

It may be appropriate for a judge at the start of a sentencing circle to outline the constraints upon his or her ability to adopt recommendations put forward by the circle. This was done in a sentencing circle that I participated in as defence counsel, where the judge clearly set out the parameters placed on him by the *Criminal Code.*[28] This circle was considering whether an offender, who had plead guilty to impaired driving, would be granted a conditional discharge for curative treatment. This sentence, if granted, would compel him into inpatient alcohol treatment but would avoid an otherwise mandatory jail sentence. Judge Diehl of the Provincial Court of Saskatchewan clearly set out the sentence he would be compelled to impose if the circle was not able to convince him that a conditional discharge was appropriate for this offender. Although such an explanation by a judge may not be understood or accepted by all in attendance, circle participants will be less likely to believe they have been deceived if a circle consensus is subsequently rejected by the judge.

Despite the potential for confusion, community members play a real part in the ultimate sentencing decision. Although the judge possesses the legal right and obligation to impose sentence, in reality, the sentencing decision is not always "made" by the judge. Of the sixty to seventy sentencing circles conducted by Judge Fafard in northern Saskatchewan by the winter of 1994, he claimed never to have rejected a circle consensus and believed that, as a result, community members were enjoying a significant role in decision making at court:

> [The community] may not have the final say because I can't give it to them, but I'm giving them a role in the decision-making process and they're genuinely getting to believe that, if it's within reason, I won't interfere with it because I never have interfered with it. I've never had reason to disagree with a [sentencing] recommendation.[29]

It is important not to underestimate the effect of allowing local community members to participate in the court process. Judges are human and are likely to be receptive to representations that focus on local aspirations and perspectives. The formal justice system cannot function in a vacuum; it must find some measure of credibility and respectability with the local citizens it controls. In the context of a sentencing circle, it is unlikely a judge would disregard a circle consensus that proposed a viable alternative to the sentence that would otherwise have been imposed. To do so would undoubtedly risk a loss of credibility by the court in the eyes of the local community.

What is meant by word "consensus," however, is not entirely clear. During my study I found no clear indication of the extent of agreement required to constitute a circle consensus. Lawyer Robin Ritter, in summarizing the practice of circle sentencing in northern Saskatchewan, equated consensus with unanimity.[30] However, the circle in *Morin*[31] showed a "consensus without unanimity," as the Crown prosecutor actively opposed the proposed sentence. In all the sentencing circles I studied in Saskatchewan— at Sandy Bay, Cumberland House, and Pelican Narrows—the Crown, represented by a prosecutor or the RCMP, was in agreement with the consensus reached by other circle members. In one instance, Constable Murray Bartley of Cumberland House did advise that he was unhappy with the result of a sentencing circle held for a young offender; however, it was not clear whether he verbally opposed the circle consensus at the sentencing circle.[32] The frequency of consensus within Saskatchewan circles was partly due to the reluctance of judges to conduct circles in the face of opposition from the Crown.[33]

To require unanimity within all sentencing circles appears to be unrealistic, given the potential for a recalcitrant participant to obstruct an otherwise acceptable and workable recommendation. This point was stressed by Chief Justice Bayda in *Morin,* who said that an "intransigent participant who, it turns out, may have motives inconsistent with the success or effectiveness of a sentencing circle should not be the holder of what amounts to a veto on the proceedings."[34] Whether unanimous or not, a viable consensus appears to depend on the active support of community representatives, including the victim, the Crown, the police, the offender, and the judge. All sentencing circles are open to the public and, as a result, people with no interest in the specific cases or knowledge of the offenders or victims involved can participate. It is therefore doubtful that solitary opposition by such a community member would nullify a consensus of all other circle participants.

Related to consideration of legal status is the question of what limits should be put on circle sentencing. Specifically, what offender and offences should be allowed to come before a sentencing circle?

Criteria for Circle Sentencing

Circle sentencing requires a considerable expenditure of court time and resources. In *R. v. Johnson,*[35] Justice Finch of the Yukon Court of Appeal expressed concern over the absence of criteria controlling the selection of circle sentencing cases:

> Sentencing circles [as] employed in this case took far longer than the sentencing process prescribed in the *Criminal Code* and it was apparent that this process could not be used in every case. . . . If judges proposed to use sentencing circles, they should establish and publish rules so that the Crown and the accused would know the kinds of cases to be tried in that way and what to expect. . . . It would be wrong if judges of the court should follow different procedures on such a common question as sentencing.[36]

Time limitations place significant restrictions on the use of circle sentencing. The sentencing circles considered in this study each took at least two hours. Heavy schedules are common in many rural and northern courts. Constable Murray Bartley of Cumberland House described a court docket day that included twenty-two accused appearing before the court on a total of thirty-five charges. He considered this to be moderate. He said as many as five to six trials may be scheduled for trial days.[37] In my work as defence counsel in rural courts across central and northern Saskatchewan, I have witnessed many sittings where more than fifty accused have appeared before the court. At these sittings, the court has dealt with a variety of matters, including receiving pleas from accused, sentencing offenders, deciding whether prisoners are to be released on bail, and conducting trials or pre-liminary hearings. Given these substantial demands on the court system, and assuming no substantial increase in court resources or available time for court sittings, time considerations will necessitate the selective use of circle sentencing.

One way to address the limited time available for sentencing circles is for judges to establish written guidelines restricting the range of cases that may be concluded in this fashion. In an effort to narrow this range, Judge Fafard, in *R.* v. *Joseyounen,* set out the following criteria:

1.   The accused must agree to be referred to the sentencing circle.
2.   The accused must have deep roots in the community in which the circle is held and from which the participants are drawn.
3.   There are elders or respected non-political community leaders willing to participate.
4.   The victim is willing to participate and has been subjected to no coercion or pressure in so agreeing.
5.   The court should try to determine beforehand, as best it can, if the victim is subject to battered woman's syndrome. If she is, then she should have counseling and be accompanied by a support team in the circle.
6.   Disputed facts have been resolved in advance.
7.   The case is one which a court would be willing to take a calculated risk and depart from the usual range of sentencing.[38]

These criteria have been widely quoted and applied across Canada.

Time constraints, although significant, are not the only concern prompt-ing development of formal guidelines. Judge Fafard explained his motiva-tion:

> In deciding whether or not to hold a sentencing circle the court is exercising a judicial function. That means the decision must not be made arbitrarily; it must be made with reference to certain criteria. Those criteria must be such that the public can be made aware of them. A democratic society cannot suffer a situation where a reasonably well-informed person with the application of due diligence cannot discover what rule (what law) is being applied. . . . These

criteria are not carved in stone, but they provide guidelines sufficiently simple for lay people to understand and [are] also capable of application so that our decisions are not being made arbitrarily. It is imperative that the public, aboriginal and others[,] be able to know what is happening in the development of sentencing circles: the credibility of the administration of justice depends on it.[39]

Although not defining the bounds of circle sentencing to this extent, Judge Desjardins in *Nicholas*,[40] Justice Milliken in *Morin*,[41] and Judge Dutil in *R. v. Aluka*[42] viewed as prerequisites a desire for rehabilitation by the offender and a community prepared to provide offender assistance and support during and after sentencing. In the appeal judgement of *Morin*,[43] Justice Sherstobitoff refused to lay down specific guidelines governing the decision to form a sentencing circle but did comment that the criteria employed by Justice Milliken at trial-level sentencing "could apply to almost any case."[44]

A related issue in choosing cases for circle sentencing is whether a guilty plea is a prerequisite. Should an offender who pleads not guilty and proceeds through a trial be entitled to a sentencing circle? In *Joseyounen*, Judge Fafard argued that a guilty plea was necessary:

> [T]he strongest indication of remorse is a guilty plea. It would be difficult to discover genuine remorse in an individual who has pled "not guilty", had his trial and after conviction says, "Now that you have found me guilty I am full of remorse and I want to mend my ways." It smacks of "death bed repentance", especially where the accused has testified that his conduct was not wrongful.[45]

Not surprisingly, requests for sentencing circles after trial have been strenuously opposed by Crown prosecutors. This situation arose in *Taylor*.[46] The offender maintained throughout his trial that he had not sexually assaulted the victim and that she had consented to sexual intercourse. The victim adamantly denied this. After a guilty verdict, the offender applied for a sentencing circle. On appeal, Chief Justice Bayda stressed the significance of a guilty plea, which, he said, was "usually a good measure of an accused's accepting responsibility for his wrongdoing and his sincerity to be restored in his relationship with the community and the victims of the wrongdoing."[47] In the *Taylor* case, however, the majority of the Saskatchewan Court of Appeal held that a not-guilty plea does "not necessarily preclude the holding of a sentencing circle" but said it does "require the offender to demonstrate his remorse, sincerity and acceptance of responsibility in some other way."[48] It is difficult to understand how a sentencing circle could be appropriate for an offender who maintains his or her innocence after trial.

This is especially true considering the allocation of already scarce court time and community resources required to conduct a sentencing circle.

Crown support, whether for individual sentencing circle decisions or for overall community sentencing initiatives, is an important consideration in the selection of cases for circle sentencing. Judge Robert Kopstein of the Provincial Court of Manitoba, who facilitated the involvement of local elders in the sentencing process at Rousseau River, Manitoba, during the 1970s, recognized the importance of Crown support for such initiatives.[49] In the Yukon, Crown agreement also appears to have been important, as Justice Hudson of the Yukon Territory Supreme Court commented in *R.* v. *Lucas* that "this was not a sentencing circle in the cultural sense that has been adopted in other courts; but those are achieved [with] some preparation and the agreement of the prosecuting authorities, which was not the case here."[50]

Constable Brian Brennan of Sandy Bay stressed the necessity of Crown and victim agreement prior to formation of a sentencing circle in that community:

> If the Crown opposes it, that's it. . . . [B]asically the police are the only ones that are in . . . possession of all the evidence. They know exactly what took place and how the victim feels and if the victim says, "I don't want to do a sentencing circle, I'm terrified," say, of the guy that assaulted him, then as the Crown, we have to represent that victim, and if we take the position that we oppose it, that's it. It has to be a majority. Everybody has to be on the same wavelength, same consensus. There's not much sense in me representing the Crown at a sentencing circle where I don't think I should be and I think this guy should be sentenced according to case law by the judge because I know he's going to get x number of years. But if he goes before the sentencing circle, and he's an intimidation in a small community, no-one's going to sit there knowing that, well, we better not give this fellow too much jail time, because he's going to come back and there'll be retaliation and stuff. . . . If you have one group that is uncomfortable with the process, then it loses its mandate and it's just not going to work. There has to be some checks and balances and I think if the Crown opposes it, it shouldn't be done.[51]

This passage also points out a concern about intimidation by offenders and whether a sentencing circle can succeed without an open exchange of viewpoints and information.

An alternative to court-directed selection criteria has been protocol negotiation between communities and provincial departments of justice. One example is the Protocol of the Katapamisuak Society at the Poundmaker Cree Nation in Saskatchewan.[52] This protocol incorporated the criteria later set out by Judge Fafard in *Joseyounen*[53] and established a local justice committee to screen sentencing circle requests from offenders, police, Crown prosecutors, and judges. Another example is the Protocol for Manitoba Department of Justice Support for the Community Approach of the Hollow Water Community Holistic Circle Healing in Manitoba.[54] Although not specifically dealing with circle sentencing criteria, this protocol established guidelines for Crown consideration of community-based sentences for sex abusers and facilitated the introduction of circle sentencing at Hollow Water.

These protocols are one of the few ways local justice committees can exercise some measure of control over the types of offences chosen for circle sentencing within their communities and, it is to be hoped, some control over the sentences determined. With the ever-present pressure of provincewide sentence parity, such protocols give some assurance to communities that the Crown will not appeal a sentence that is in compliance with the protocol. This was clearly the result at Hollow Water, where a number of sexual assault cases resulted in suspended sentences with the support of the Crown. There is little doubt that the Manitoba Court of Appeal would have found a substantial penitentiary term appropriate for these offences, had it been called upon to rule on these cases.

Sentencing circles have considered a wide range of serious offences, including aggravated assault,[55] assault causing bodily harm,[56] robbery with violence,[57] sexual assault,[58] spousal assault,[59] criminal harassment,[60] impaired driving causing death,[61] break and enter,[62] theft over $1,000,[63] and arson.[64] Although the personal circumstances of an offender have been an element considered in sentencing, appellate court guidelines may restrict the range of offences referred to sentencing circles. Justice Grotsky of the Saskatchewan Court of Queen's Bench, in *R. v. Cheekinew*,[65] emphasized, in considering a sentencing circle request by an offender found guilty of aggravated assault, that the *Criminal Code* did not permit a term of probation to follow a penitentiary term of more than two years and therefore a sentencing circle request would be inappropriate for an offender facing a certain penitentiary term. As Justice Sherstobitoff stated in *Morin*,[66] "[I]t would be futile . . . to use a sentencing circle for those cases where it is clear that the circumstances require, at a minimum, a penitentiary term."[67]

This line of reasoning suggests that sentencing circle participants have no role to play if probation is not a possible outcome of the conventional sentencing process. Although Judge Stuart, in *Moses,* recognized that the "circle may not be appropriate for all crimes,"[68] is it possible to predetermine the appropriateness of circle sentencing simply on the basis of the offence committed, without considering the specific circumstances of both the offence and the offender? Certainly, judicial adherence to starting-point sentences for such offences as sexual assault[69] will restrict the use of sentencing circles. However, in response to the suggestion that some cases may be predetermined as unsuitable for circle sentencing simply due to estab-lished sentencing tariffs, Professor Tim Quigley argued that, except in obvious cases such as homicide, the broad discretion open to a sentencing judge makes it difficult to predetermine what and how long a sentence should be:

> [T]hese restrictions [on circle sentencing] put the cart before the horse. It is only during the process itself that it can be learned whether the offender is remorseful and motivated to change, whether the community is willing to provide the necessary support and, perhaps most fundamentally, what is the appropriate sentence for this offender.[70]

Similarly, Judge Desjardins, in *Nicholas,* rejected that notion that sentencing circles be used only for offences where the normal range of sentence is less than two years. He viewed "the nature of [an] offence and possible range of sentence" as factors to be considered in, but not as determinative of, a sentencing circle application.[71]

This discussion once again brings into question the effect of appellate court guidance on appropriate sentencing ranges and starting-point sentences. These topics were reviewed at length by the Supreme Court of Canada in *McDonnell,*[72] a sexual assault case from Alberta. Although he acknowledged the propriety of appellate starting-point sentences for specific offences, Supreme Court Justice Sopinka, speaking for the majority, held that an appellate court should not interfere with a lower court's sentence unless that sentence was demonstrably unfit. Deviation from an appellate starting point was said to be one factor in considering unfitness but, failing a finding of demonstrable unfitness, Justice Sopinka felt that this deviation should not result in appellate intervention.

Although the implications of appellate sentencing tariffs are obvious, other factors may also influence the decision to conduct a sentencing circle. For example, in cases of domestic violence there are often long-standing power imbalances between offenders and victims. Feminist scholars, in particular, have questioned the application of mediation to family law cases involving wife abuse. Given the ubiquity of domestic violence, mediation in criminal offences and the meeting of offender and victim in a sentencing circle may be problematic. Martha Shaffer has argued that long-standing power imbalances are not easily overcome:

> Since experts estimate that one in three women is battered by her spouse, the problem of mediating domestic violence cases is not insignificant. It is dif-ficult to imagine a situation in which the power imbalance between the spouses is more pronounced and the potential consequences of mediation more dis-astrous. It is grossly unrealistic to assume that women who have been sub-

jected to a pattern of repeated abuse will suddenly be able to face their abuser[s].[73]

Justice Co-ordinator Mary Crnkovich described an example of such a power imbalance within an Inuit sentencing circle in northern Quebec. This circle had been formed to consider the sentence of an offender who had assaulted his wife:

> Aside from the fact that the sentence was based on a proposal presented by the accused, the victim could hardly, in her position, oppose such a proposal or complain that it was not working. Again to suggest that her attendance [for counselling] would keep the accused honest, demonstrates, in the author's view, the judge's misunderstanding of the life circumstances of this woman as a victim of violence. How could this woman speak out against her husband? How could she speak out against the mayor [and] . . . others in her community [who attended the sentencing circle]? Did the judge really believe she would speak out based on the history of this case to date? The victim's actions or lack thereof during the circle, demonstrated the degree of fear and deference paid to her spouse.[74]

Rupert Ross has suggested that it might be inappropriate to conduct a sentencing circle without previously identifying and addressing power imbalances between offenders and victims.[75] This appears not to have been done in the Inuit circle described above. Such an approach was, however, practised at Hollow Water in cases of serious child sexual abuse. At Hollow Water, each offender and victim was assigned a separate support team, and the two were not brought together until such time as they could face each other on an equal footing.[76] When a sentencing circle was held, the victim was encouraged, but not required, to attend. If the victim chose to attend the circle, he or she was accompanied by a specific worker for support.[77]

The Hollow Water approach brings into question the appropriateness of circle sentencing for cases involving domestic violence unless there has been prior intervention by a local justice committee or other local support personnel. Intervention prior to sentencing, however, means lengthy adjournments of sentencing by the trial court. At Hollow Water, there was a protocol in effect between the Manitoba Department of Justice and the community that recognized the propriety of such adjournments for completion of the healing program. However, the Alberta Court of Appeal, in *R. v. A.B.C.*,[78] rejected the practice of lengthy adjournments for treatment, making the Hollow Water approach unlikely to be accepted in Alberta. The Saskatchewan Court of Appeal, in *Taylor*,[79] also rejected the trial judge's decision, following a sentencing circle, to adjourn sentencing for one year and to banish the offender

to an isolated island under the terms of an undertaking. If lengthy adjournments are sought, for such purposes as facilitating victim counselling and
support prior to a sentencing circle, Crown consent is essential. If this support
is not forthcoming, lengthy adjournments will likely be declared unlawful
if contested on appeal.

In contrast to domestic assault cases, sentencing circles may be more
beneficial, and potentially less threatening, when victims not well acquainted
with the offenders.[80] In *Morin*,[81] the victim and offender were strangers prior
to the offence. The sentencing circle appears to have allowed the victim to
confront her assailant while putting a human face to him. At the circle, she
directly challenged the offender, Ivan Morin:

> Morin's victim, [a] university student . . . said she didn't hate Morin and didn't
> appear [to be] looking for revenge. "I did not come here out of vindictiveness
> and I have no anger towards you. I came here to challenge you in your actions."
> [The victim] said what she and the rest of the community wanted was a
> commitment from Morin to break his cycle of crime. "I need a commitment
> from you to better yourself. It can't come from anyone else here," [the victim]
> said.[82]

This victim also attained insight into the offender's personal situation and
problems.[83]

Although reconciliation between parties to an offence is possible during
a sentencing circle, offences involving long-standing power imbalances will
continue to necessitate vigilance by judges in ensuring, to the extent possible, protection of the victims. Unfortunately, such protection may be short-
lived in isolated communities, where the routine departure of the court party
after adjournment makes community-based support for such victims essential. Cases of domestic violence underscore the importance of ongoing resources and support at the local level for both victims and offenders. It is
unrealistic to expect that a few hours in a sentencing circle will permanently
alter historic patterns of offending and imbalances of power. Clearly, sentencing circles can be catalysts to start significant changes in behaviour on
the part of offenders. Any chance of achieving this goal, however, depends
on the availability and success of locally accessible resources, including
support, treatment, and counselling for victims and offenders, and, in cases
involving abuse, close supervision of offenders and protection of victims.

The appropriateness of community participation at sentencing may also
bring into question the treatment of the victim by the local community as
a whole. Caution respecting power imbalances between offenders and victims, in the context of a request for a community-based sentencing hearing,
was expressed by the Ontario Court of Justice (General Division) in *R.* v.

A.F. The victim had been outcast from her community as a result of her complaint and the resulting criminal proceeding. She had moved to southern Ontario following her disclosure. Justice Stach voiced the following caution:

> The success of a community-based sentencing approach depends very much upon the active participation of and sincere commitment of each participant. . . . So too, where the nature of the crime bespeaks an imbalance of power as between the victim and the offender, great care ought to be taken. . . . The perspective of the accused, the convenience of witnesses and the perspective of the community are not the only considerations. The rights of the public, the perspective of the victim, and the Court's duty to ascertain the truth are all competing and sometime competing considerations. In cases of sexual assault, for example, an imbalance of power as between the offender and the victim is commonplace. Where the imbalance is not offset by some other visible community support for the victim, the logic of a community-based sentencing hearing is dissipated.[84]

Questions of power imbalance highlight the complex dynamics that may occur during a sentencing circle. A related aspect is the effect that community members and the victim have on an offender during a sentencing circle. This question is considered in detail in the following section.

Deterrence through Circle Sentencing

A central goal of sentencing in Canadian law has been deterrence, both specific and general.[85] Section 718(b) of the *Criminal Code* now provides that an objective of sentencing is to "deter the offender and other persons from committing offences." Although incarceration has been the predominant means of achieving deterrence within the prevailing system, Judge Stuart, in *R.* v. *Washpan,* commented that community-based options also deter crime:

> A severe sentence is not the only punitive sanction that serves to achieve general deterrence. Other forms of punishment, either in lieu of jail or in addition to jail, depending upon the crime, offender and community, may be as effective in achieving general deterrence and at the same time be less disruptive of other sentencing objectives.[86]

Community members at Hollow Water argued that deterrence of sexual offences could be accomplished more effectively without jail, as jail terms reinforce silence and promote the cycle of violence by reducing disclosures of abuse. The Hollow Water Assessment Team expressed their frustration in this fashion:

The legal system's use of incarceration under the guise of specific and general deterrence also seems, to us, to be ineffective in breaking the cycle of violence. Victimization has become so much a part of who we are, as a people and a community, that the threat of jail simply does not deter offending behaviour. What the threat of incarceration does is keep people from coming forward and taking responsibility for the hurt they are causing. It reinforces the silence and therefore promotes, rather than breaks, the cycle of violence that exists. In reality, rather than making the community a safer place, the threat of jail places the community more at risk.[87]

Berma Bushie of Hollow Water stated that incarceration provides no treatment for offenders and has failed to deter sexual abuse:

When a person is incarcerated . . . they return, thinking that they've paid their price for their crime. And the chance of re-offending is very high, because there's no treatment, absolutely no treatment in the jail system for offenders. And why I say that is because one offender that was incarcerated and was willing to work with us . . . sat in jail under the pretence of some traffic violations. And so how could he deal with his crime . . . when he has to pretend that he's in there for something totally innocent. So that's the reason why we don't want our people going to jail. And they come back thinking they've done their [time], they've paid for the crime, and in most cases we have no way of working with these people because it would have to be totally voluntary on the offender's part [after release].[88]

The effectiveness of jail as a means of deterring crime has been widely questioned. These criticisms have necessitated the search for other means of achieving deterrence. The mere presence of community members within in a circle has been shown to have an effect on offenders and to deter further deviant behaviour. In *D.N.,* Judge Stuart commented that "as any offender who has been through a [Sentencing] Circle and community rehabilitation sentence will attest, jail is a shorter, less demanding and less traumatic sentence."[89] The deterrent effect of circle sentencing was described by Greg Bragstad, a resident of Sandy Bay, who had participated in a number of sentencing circles:

That was the decision of the sentencing circle, and that was the community that decided that. And so it has stopped two people from doing crime because of it. . . . They [the two young offenders sentenced in the circle] haven't been in court since so that tells me they're not doing anything. . . . I think [the sentencing circle] gave them time to think about what they did and it gave them the message that the community is not going to tolerate it and, again, that gives the community some ownership—rather than just having a judge fly in and you go to jail, you do this, you do that.[90]

Shaming has been a key element in the success of the sentencing circle as deterrent. Professor John Braithwaite argued that the most effective way to deter crime in a community was through an organized form of shaming by the local community, while at the same time reintegrating offenders into that community.[91] This shaming process is likely to continue after sentencing, as recognized in *R. v. Genaille,*[92] where the court, although not considering a sentence arrived at through a sentencing circle, commented that the offender would be returning to his Aboriginal community, who would continue to remind him of the offence.

Although there is judicial disagreement on how specific and general deterrence might best be accomplished, judges such as Stuart in the Yukon and Fafard in Saskatchewan have recognized the power of local Aboriginal communities to deter criminal behaviour. Working within the prevailing legal system, these judges have used judicial discretion in sentencing to tap into local systems of social control, thereby accessing additional resources in their attempts to change offender behaviour. In my own work with a large number of Aboriginal offenders in courts across northeastern Saskatchewan, I have observed the positive effects of family ties and community support on these people. Although most offenders show respect for the formal court process when appearing before a judge, a long-term change in behaviour is far more likely to be effected through the intervention and support of close family and community members. Involving these people to the greatest extent possible during sentencing makes obvious sense.

Circle Sentencing at Hollow Water, Manitoba
Community Overview

Hollow Water is located 190 kilometres (118 miles) northeast of Winnipeg on the east shore of Lake Winnipeg. It covers 1620 hectares (4,000 acres) of land within the Canadian Precambrian Shield. The band's native language is Ojibway. As of 1994, the on-reserve population was 490 and off-reserve was 512. This band is a signatory to Treaty 5, signed in 1875.[93] Hollow Water is bordered by the Metis communities of Aghaming, Manigotogan, and Seymourville. The total resident population of Hollow Water and the surrounding communities is 1200.[94] Resources at Hollow Water include a K–12 school, a convenience store, a gas bar, a community hall, a band office, and a water treatment plant. No regular court sittings are held at Hollow Water. Provincial Court for this community is held 100 kilometres (62 miles) to the south in Pine Falls. However, since December of 1993, the Provincial Court of Manitoba has convened at Hollow Water to conduct sentencing circles that have dealt with offenders charged with sexual assault.[95]

Introduction and Development of Circle Sentencing

Hollow Water represents a unique example of a community-driven approach to dispute resolution and the healing and treatment of both offenders and victims. Rupert Ross described its development:

> In 1984, a group of social service providers got together, concerned about the future of their young people. As they looked into the issues of youth substance abuse, vandalism, truancy and suicide, their focus shifted to the home life of those children and to the substance abuse and family violence that often prevailed. Upon closer examination of those issues, the focus changed again, for inter-generational sexual abuse was identified as the root problem. Other dysfunctional behaviour came to be seen primarily as symptomatic. By 1987, they began to tackle sexual abuse head on, creating what they have called their Community Holistic Circle Healing Program [CHCH]. They presently estimate that 75 percent of the population of Hollow Water are victims of sexual abuse, and 35 percent are "victimizers."[96]

CHCH co-ordinator Berma Bushie cited frustration with the prevailing criminal justice and child welfare systems as factors contributing to CHCH's development:

> We also studied the *Child Welfare Act,* the legal system and how it was dealing with these [child sexual abuse] cases, and we were horrified to find out that our children were further victimized. . . . Child Welfare's practice at the time, and probably still is, is when a child disclosed [he or she was] . . . removed from the family and, in a lot of situations, a child was removed from the community. And then there's absolutely no help offered to the offender. Everything was turned over to the legal system and charges laid, court would take place, and that's it. And the child would be expected to testify against the offender in criminal court, and to us that's not protecting our children. So based on the laws that continue to govern us, we feel that we have to ensure protection for our children. We have to have a say in what happens to them.[97]

As of February 6, 1995, the assessment team comprised seven sexual abuse workers, the local child and family service supervisor, a support worker, a councillor from the band, two Native Alcohol (NADAP) workers, a public health nurse, a local band constable, an RCMP officer from Pine Falls, a person from the Roman Catholic church, two people from provincial Child and Family Services, and the local school principal. The procedure followed by CHCH's assessment team is complex and includes provision of support and treatment for victims and victimizers and their respective families.[98]

After initial disclosure of sexual abuse by a child, a thirteen-step process is followed by the assessment team. These steps are: (1) effecting disclosure, (2) protecting the child/victim, (3) confronting the victimizer, (4) assisting the victimizer's spouse, (5) assisting the family or families directly affected and the community, (6) calling together the assessment team, (7) getting the victimizer to admit and accept responsibility, (8) preparing the victimizer, (9) preparing the victim, (10) preparing all family or families, (11) organizing a special gathering, (12) implementing the healing contract, and (13) conducting the cleansing ceremony.[99]

The assessment team is divided into support teams for the victim, victimizer, and family.[100] After ensuring the safety of the victim, the accused is confronted by a member of the assessment team, who encourages the accused to take responsibility for his or her actions and to participate in CHCH. Berma Bushie explained:

> We feel as a community it's our job to go and confront the offender and not to rely on the RCMP because they haven't been very successful in getting people to take responsibility for what they've done. When people see the RCMP, they just clam up, won't speak, and so we feel as a community we have a better . . . track record of getting people to take responsibility for what they've done. . . . Nine times out of ten, the offender takes responsibility, and we inform the offender of the plan in place. We inform [him] of the community approach. We also inform him about the treatment expectations, the circles that . . . he's going to have to go through. We also tell the offender that he has to go plead guilty in court.[101]

When criminal charges follow a disclosure, the CHCH approach promotes acceptance of responsibility by the offender through entry of an early guilty plea in court. This practice stands in sharp contrast to the presumption of innocence enjoyed by accused persons in Canadian law and their right to remain silent. In fairness, though, the goal of team members is to help both child complainants and adult accused. After entry of a guilty plea, members of the assessment team then ask the court to adjourn sentencing for at least four months to allow treatment with the offender to begin. Berma Bushie indicated that this period of time was requested so that the assessment team could be assured that the offender was committed to healing.

Offenders are expected to participate in four circles. In the first circle, the offender discloses details of his offence to the CHCH assessment team. In the second circle, the victim tells the offender how the abuse has affected his or her life. In the third circle, the offender describes his actions to his family. Finally, in the fourth circle, the offender faces his community in a sentencing circle.[102] Prior to the introduction of circle sentencing at Hollow Water in December 1993, the assessment team prepared and presented recommendations on sentence to the court sitting in Pine Falls. This procedure was outlined in *R. v. S.(H.M.)*.[103]

CHCH has actively opposed offender incarceration and has argued that jail cannot break the generational cycle of violence.[104] Assessment team member Marcel Hardesty supported this analysis.[105] He explained that he had asked a sexual offender, recently returned from jail, whether he would commit the offence again. The offender had responded that he would be sure not to get caught if he did it again. Hardesty questioned the lesson being taught by jail and suggested incarceration only reduces the chances of other victims and abusers coming forward.

CHCH focusses on restoring harmony between victims and offenders and the community-at-large through traditional holistic practices. In this process, a conjunctive relationship has developed between CHCH and the criminal justice system both prior to and after sentencing.[106] A protocol between the Manitoba Department of Justice and CHCH was negotiated in 1991 in which the department recognized CHCH's program as an option for the treatment and supervision of sexual assault offenders and agreed to consider a non-custodial sentence if that was the recommendation of the assessment team.[107] This protocol was negotiated by CHCH to give the assessment team input into sentencing and to avoid repeatedly educating Crown attorneys about the CHCH approach.[108]

The first sentencing circle at Hollow Water occurred December 9, 1993.[109] It involved serious sexual assaults perpetrated by two parents on their children. The assessment team foresaw dire consequences for the offenders if this case went through the conventional system. According to assessment team member Lorne Hagel, Judge Murray Sinclair of the Provincial Court of Manitoba had advised the team that, given the offences and circumstances involved, eight to ten years' incarceration would be a realistic sentence. Judge Sinclair advised me that the initial Crown position on sentence was five to six years' incarceration, while even defence counsel conceded that two-and-a-half to four years might be appropriate for one offender, with less jail time for the other.[110] The CHCH assessment team made representations to the Provincial Court requesting formation of a sentencing circle and explaining the evolution of community participation in that community. The submission characterized circle sentencing as an extension of the community's role in holding offenders accountable for their actions and healing the pain they inflicted on their victims:

Up until now the sentencing hearing has been the point at which all of the parties of the legal system (Crown, defence, judge) and the community have come together. Major differences of opinion as to how to proceed have often existed. As we see it, the legal system usually arrives with an outside agenda of punishment and deterrence of the "guilty" victimizer, and safety and protection of the victim and community; the community on the other hand, arrives with an agenda of accountability of the victimizer to the community, and restoration of balance to all parties of the victimization.

As we see it, the differences in the agendas are seriously deterring the healing process of the community. We believe that the restoration of balance is more likely to occur if sentencing itself is more consistent in process and in content with the healing work of the community. Sentencing needs to become more of a step in the healing process, rather than a diversion from it. . . . The sentencing circle promotes the above rationale. . . . As we see it, the sentencing circle plays two primary purposes (1) it promotes the community healing process by providing a forum for the community to address the parties at the time of sentencing, and (2) it allows the court to hear directly from the people most directly affected by the pain of the victimization. In the past the Crown and defence, as well as ourselves, have attempted to portray this information. We believe that it is now time for the court to hear from the victim, the family of the victim, the victimizer, the family of the victimizer and the community-at-large.[111]

This first sentencing circle commenced at seven o'clock in the morning with a sunrise and pipe ceremony and ended at nine o'clock that night.[112] *Winnipeg Free Press* reporter Kevin Rollason described the atmosphere and process followed at this circle:

While the smell of sweet grass filled the air, two circles were formed in the centre of the hall for the sentencing of a man and woman charged with incest. The inner circle of about 40 people held the key participants—including both offenders and victims—while the outer circle consisted of about 200 other relatives, friends and community members. . . . Just before court was called to order, a man holding a tray of burning sweet grass and buffalo grass went around the inner circle, allowing each participant to "wash" the smoke over their hair, faces and clothes. Passing an eagle feather from hand to hand, each person spoke in order around the circles. The discussion went around a total of four times. During the first circle, people spoke about why they were there. During the second, participants were able to speak to the victims. The third and fourth circles were designed to be separate—one centering on the effects of the crime and the other on "restoring balance" to the offenders. However, when the proceedings threatened to extend well into the night, the last two circles had to be melded into one.[113]

At the conclusion of the circle, all participants, with the exception of a cousin of one of the victims but including the Crown prosecutor, agreed jail would be counterproductive for these offenders. Judge Sinclair indicated to me that these offenders had progressed from a state of total denial to one of total acceptance and responsibility for their actions. In addition, the two had actively worked in convincing one hundred other sexual abusers from Hollow Water to come forward and admit their actions publicly.[114] At the circle's conclusion, Judge Sinclair imposed a three-year suspended sentence on each offender with probation containing a condition that each offender follow the directions of the CHCH assessment team.

Despite the many disclosures of abuse heard at the initial Hollow Water sentencing circle, few subsequent sentencing circles were conducted and there was no increase in sexual assault charges laid against Hollow Water residents. This suggests that many incidents of abuse were being dealt with locally outside the conventional justice system or were not being dealt with at all. An article on Hollow Water published on April 8, 1995, in the *Globe and Mail* stated that, since 1986, only five offenders had been jailed instead of entering the CHCH program and forty-eight offenders had enrolled in the treatment program.[115]

The limited number of offenders sentenced through sentencing circles or incarcerated outside the CHCH program suggest that many offenders in the program were not being charged. This highlights the interesting and often-complex relationship between local dispute-resolution processes and the broader justice system. At one level, the community of Hollow Water was working conjunctively with the formal justice system, through the involvement of CHCH members in court assessments and circle sentencing. At another level, the community was apparently operating separately from the formal system, assuming complete control of dispute resolution. The reality across the criminal justice system in Canada is that the number of cases processed through the formal system represents only a small proportion of ongoing criminal activity. What may be different at Hollow Water is the availability of local resources to address the behaviour of offenders, while at the same time protecting victims within that community.

As part of their local system of social control, and in an effort to hold offenders responsible for their actions and encourage their active participation in treatment, a community review was held on the six-month anniversary of each sentencing circle. Berma Bushie explained:

One of the things that the community does is, after sentencing, we tell the offenders "for the next three years, you are on probation and every six months we are bringing the case back to the community, for the community to review how you are doing in treatment. . . ." [The community review] is one of the ways, besides probation, . . . used to make sure that people are following the [sentencing circle's] recommendation.[116]

The review process encourages community assistance in holding offenders accountable for their victimization and promotes active participation in their treatment. As Bushie explained:

> We found that after the first sentencing circle back in December 1993 . . . that in the treatment area . . . there was a regression on the part of the offenders. They were getting back into their denial process. They were getting back to creating negative support for their case and stuff like that. . . . [W]e felt that . . . [our assessment] team was not strong enough to stop the regression and to get the people [offenders] back on track with their healing. And because the community came out to speak and give recommendations to the court for their sentencing [circle] . . . we felt as a team . . . we needed to go back to the community to report . . . what was happening. . . . And as a team we felt that, before we thought about going through [the process of charging the offenders with breach of] probation and bringing this case back to court, . . . we felt that we . . . should go back through the community. First, give all the details . . . and have the community help us decide where this case should go. . . . And they [the community members in attendance at the review] felt that these people should be given a chance, and that, again, they repeated their support for these people. They repeated their expectations of the kinds of treatments they wanted the offenders to take, and the work that they wanted them to do. And we said, "Okay, we'll do that and six months down the line, we'll come back and we'll report to you and see how these people are doing."[117]

A community sentencing review held at Hollow Water on February 22, 1995,[118] for three sexual offenders who had been sentenced through a sentencing circle was attended by approximately thirty community members, including one of the victims. The victim in attendance had been victimized by two of the offenders. She was apparently sitting in a circle with her abusers for the first time, although she did not speak. The other victim had moved to Winnipeg. The assessment team members assigned to each victim and offender were present and reported to the circle.

This review followed a similar format to the sentencing circles. During successive rounds of the circle, participants in the review learned of the treatment and progress of all victims and offenders and, in turn, addressed the three offenders and one victim in attendance. Participants also developed recommendations for continued offender treatment and victim support. Comments by participants made it clear there was strong community pressure on the offenders to continue treatment. Several women, while acknowledging the progress made by each offender, openly challenged the offenders not to regress in their treatment and to assist the assessment team by naming their other victims. Berma Bushie commented to the offenders that jail "would have been the easy way out for you." She thanked them for taking responsibility for their actions and for facing their community in the circle.

Perspectives of Community Members and Justice System Personnel on Developments at Hollow Water

CHCH's development provides an interesting insight into local community dynamics and perspectives on justice. Initially, the CHCH assessment team members became very unpopular within the community as many people blamed them for raising painful memories. Berma Bushie referred to this period as the "crucifixion":

> I would say [the "crucifixion" lasted] about the first five years, from '86 to '91. I think it took our community that time to finally accept that this problem is here, that many, many of our people have been affected by sexual abuse, and that it continued to affect our children, and once our community was able to focus on the children, then they couldn't deny the problem any more. And our children I feel more than once have saved our community because they're the ones that began to disclose about current situations and through that process it helped our community begin to accept the problem because they could not deny the children. They could deny us, the adults, trying to break the cycle. But the children helped the community accept the problem and begin to look at ways of dealing with it at the community level.[119]

Although CHCH has come to enjoy significant public support, Bushie described its dynamic relationship with the Hollow Water community:

> We find that we cannot leave our community behind. Why I say that is in the last two years, our team has concentrated on developing the treatment and making sure that was solid and in place. And so . . . we did not have the time to work on the community piece. What we used to do was a lot of workshops, just keeping that consciousness open, and teaching the adults and there was a lot of group work being done. So there was a lot of prevention aspects to our work. In the last one and a half years, we haven't been able to do that. So we've kind of left our community back there.[120]

When I interviewed her on February 6, 1995, she feared her community was slipping back into a state of denial about sexual abuse and felt that a re-emphasis on community education was required.

Assessment team member Marcel Hardesty viewed CHCH as a means of community empowerment. In his opening remarks at the Hollow Water review, he described self-government as people gaining "control over their own lives," not merely control over financial resources. Despite the close relationship between CHCH and the justice system, assessment team members believed this link should eventually be severed. Hardesty believed his community could hold abusers responsible for their actions through public awareness of specific victimizations and through the education and treatment of offenders.[121] Berma Bushie described the process she envisaged after separation from the prevailing system:

> We would use exactly the same process where the offender has to take responsibility for their action. Minus the court. That would mean . . . some kind of justice body, maybe elders, an elders' panel, elders' group, or maybe chief and council [would exist] where these people come and state their guilt, and take responsibility, and we would use exactly the same process as we have been. That's putting them through the circles, and doing the sentencing circle.[122]

She observed that local control of the justice system would allow CHCH to enforce a five-year treatment plan on offenders as opposed to the maximum probation period of three years under the *Criminal Code*. Although she noted that sexual abuse treatment was a lifetime process, she viewed five years as the amount of time required to render an offender healthy enough to become a resource to the community.

At the request of the CHCH assessment team, Judge Sinclair agreed to facilitate movement of the court to Hollow Water from Pine Falls in 1993. He also presided at two sentencing circles. When I interviewed him on January 17, 1995, he discussed the current problem of domestic abuse in many Aboriginal communities. He felt the problem arose, in part, from the oppressive practices of governments and other external systems, which had contributed to the inability of Aboriginal communities to shape appropriate social conduct for their members. Residential schools imposed institutional models on Aboriginal children that taught external control rather than internal control through development of appropriate value systems. He told me he believed a socialized dependence upon external systems of control leads to misbehaviour when such controls are removed. He also told me he believed that the current justice system has not been effective in dealing with sexual abusers from Aboriginal communities. Court proceedings take place away from the offender's community (at the Court of Queen's Bench in Winnipeg). If convicted, the offender is faced with a penitentiary term during which sexual abuse treatment rarely occurs. Upon release, he usually returns to his community without the benefit and supervision of a probation order.[123]

At the initial Hollow Water sentencing circle, Judge Sinclair agreed with the circle consensus that jail would be counterproductive for the accused. Specifically, he joined the consensus, which acknowledged:

1.   Jail would not break the cycle of abuse for the specific offenders. The only thing to be broken would be the offender's healing circle;
2.   Jail would discourage offenders in the community from coming forward for help (that is to say, there would be no incentive to participate in healing if major jail time was the result); and
3.   Jail would serve as a disincentive for victims to come forward (they are more likely to come forward if they think that their parents will not go to jail).

He noted, however, that the suspended sentences handed down after this circle were based on exceptional circumstances. He said he had met with CHCH assessment members prior to the first sentencing circle to make it clear that jail was a distinct possibility for such offences and that there could be no guarantee of suspended sentences. The CHCH assessment team, for its part, worked extensively with the offenders and their victims and provided the court with substantial documentation supporting suspended sentences. Judge Sinclair was impressed with CHCH, which he described as a community-driven, rather than a judge- or offender-driven process. The community foundation of CHCH was clearly in evidence during his first sentencing circle at Hollow Water, where he felt like an invited guest but not the focus of attention.

Crown attorney George deMoissac represented the Crown at two sentencing circles conducted at Hollow Water. He viewed CHCH as a highly trained and dedicated community-driven organization, and he felt that the protocol negotiated with the Department of Justice had the full support of local community members. It was designed for the unique circumstances of Hollow Water as a remote community with a community-based approach to addressing inter-generational sexual abuse. The CHCH assessment team had done sufficient groundwork to satisfy him, at both the sentencing circles in which he participated, that a suspended sentence would be consistent with the parameters of the protocol. Although he believed circle sentencing at Hollow Water was still in its infancy, he interpreted the community's support for this approach as being grounded in the belief that victims would be more likely to disclose abuse if they were less concerned about their abusers going to jail.[124]

Jill Duncan represented one of the offenders sentenced at the Hollow Water circle. As reported in *Canadian Lawyer,*[125] she observed that the circle melded "traditional court requirements with a healing circle." She found community participation at the sentencing circle to be a sign of strength and felt it indicated community support for this process. She viewed circle sentencing as appropriate for sexual assault charges, given what she believed to be the "learned" nature of this offence. Despite her generally positive experience at the sentencing circle, she expressed concern about the applicability of this approach outside communities such as Hollow Water. She viewed circle sentencing not as a "native/non-native issue but rather a rural/ urban issue," and she doubted that a healing circle would work in Winnipeg "because most residents don't know their neighbours."[126] She believed this approach could work in Hollow Water because "they are all long-time residents who form a tight-knit community and will be accountable for the [offenders]."[127]

The assessment team of CHCH supervised all offenders sentenced during the sentencing circles held at Hollow Water. Technically, offenders were to report both to the CHCH assessment team and to the assigned probation officer from the Department of Justice. In reality, offender supervision was conducted entirely through CHCH. Berma Bushie commented that "outside" probation officers simply did not know the resources within her community.[128] Questions surrounding the power to charge offenders with breach of probation have created some confusion within the CHCH assessment team. In February 1995, the team was considering having an offender under their supervision charged with non-compliance of a condition of his probation order; however, it appeared that the final decision rested with a probation officer from outside the reserve, suggesting that the community's powers were curtailed by requirements of the justice system.

Circle Sentencing at Sandy Bay, Saskatchewan
Community Overview

Sandy Bay is located 22 kilometres (13 miles) west of the Manitoba border and 198 kilometres (123 miles) northwest of Flin Flon, Manitoba. It is situated on the Churchill River across from Island Falls. Prior to 1927, the settlement was located a few miles downriver from the present site.[129] With the closing of the Hudson's Bay Company trading post at the old site and the opening of a store at Island Falls by Churchill Power Corporation, settlement at the current site was accelerated.[130] Drawn by the prospects of employment constructing the Island Falls power plant, people from Pelican Narrows and Cumberland House, Saskatchewan, and Pukatawagan, Manitoba, moved to Sandy Bay commencing in 1928.[131] Other than employment with the Island Falls company, people supported themselves by hunting, trapping, and fishing.[132]

Most people in Sandy Bay are Cree and speak the "th" dialect.[133]

Speakers of this dialect have been identified by various terms, including Rocky Cree, Woods Cree,[134] and Stoney Cree.[135] In 1994, the population was 1200.[136] The community has two stores, a Roman Catholic church, an RCMP detachment with three officers, a K-12 school, and a nursing station. It is connected to settlements of the South by a gravel road that is open all year.

At the time of my study, the Provincial Court convened in Sandy Bay once a month. The court party, including the judge, court clerk, and defence and Crown counsel, flew to Sandy Bay on court day and were driven to court in an RCMP vehicle. Court was held in the basement of a Roman Catholic church located in the centre of the village.[137]

Introduction and Development of Circle Sentencing

In 1992, Sandy Bay became the first Saskatchewan community to conduct a sentencing circle in court. This occurred at the suggestion of Judge Fafard with the support of community members. Harry Morin, a participant at the first sentencing circle, described the process:

> Well, we just kind of played it by ear. There was no set guidelines or nothing. We just said, "Okay, we'll deal with him, [the offender]." . . . [We got] a good mix of people, some young, middle-aged, elders, the RCMP, the magistrate, [judge], . . . the accused and his family. And we just hacked it out. . . . But, instead of looking at punishing the guy, we looked at what's causing him to do these things.[138]

Lawyer Sid Robinson described a sentencing circle held at Sandy Bay on July 22, 1992:

> Judge Fafard began his own experiment with sentencing circles in Sandy Bay . . . in cases involving [two young offenders and an adult]. For these cases, about 20 or 30 chairs were put in a circle and everyone sat down to discuss the cases at hand. The whole thing worked quite well. Judge Fafard acted as a facilitator and led most of the discussion. However, there was considerable input coming from community members with respect to each of the cases dealt with. I expect the final result in each case was similar to what Judge Fafard might have come up with on his own, but the results were definitely more of a consensus than the decision of Judge Fafard alone.[139]

Another circle, involving twenty participants, was held on August 19, 1992, for an accused who had committed arson. Robinson reported the offender "received a lot of support from community members who claimed the house he burned down was not a very good house whereas [the offender], himself, was a good fellow." The offender received a suspended sentence with probation conditions requiring alcohol treatment.[140]

By October of 1994, approximately twenty circles had been held in Sandy Bay.[141] The range of cases dealt with included assault, assault with weapon, theft under $1,000, and arson.[142] The size and makeup of the sentencing circles varied, although most included family members of the offender and victim.[143] Constable Brian Brennan noted this lack of consistency and felt circle sentencing would benefit from an established group of community members participating in all circles with only the offender, victim, and various family members changing.[144]

Perspectives of Community Members and Justice System Personnel on Developments at Sandy Bay

Perspectives on circle sentencing varied within Sandy Bay. One individual I spoke with said that sentencing circles were being used by offenders to avoid punishment and that he had been to jail "before there were sentencing circles." He believed there had to be a punishment for wrongdoing but he did not consider personal service to the victim to be a form of punishment. Despite this note of dissent, common themes emerged from other community members I interviewed.[145] Sandy Bay resident Harry Morin believed in discovering the underlying causes of deviant behaviour rather than punishing specific transgressions.[146] Verna Merasty, a participant in two sentencing circles, viewed her role as providing emotional support for the offender:

> It don't matter what kind of circle, I feel good being part of it, just to make that person [the offender] understand, we do care, because we're there for that person, just to let him know, we don't have to say anything to him, we're there for him, and sometimes he need[s] to hear that, because kids—sometimes I find children, they don't hear that at home, you're special, you're pretty, or you're a good person—so they need to hear that outside.[147]

Greg Bragstad, director of the Sandy Bay Outpatient Centre and a participant in several sentencing circles, believed circle sentencing shamed the offender and, as a result, deterred recidivism.[148]

Harry Morin identified the benefit of community supervision by community members following a circle:

> You see the nice part of it is, like, the follow-up is a lot greater . . . and you're also blocking off the breaches [of probation] because you sentence somebody, any young offender that's been addicted to something, and all of a sudden you say okay, no consumption of alcohol or drug[s] of any kind. Well, you're just setting them up. Here, locally, we can follow them up, because we know where the person lives, we keep an eye on them, and if he starts missing . . .

his counselling sessions or his appointments, then we go and check on him
and say, hey, you better get down there. That's where it's a lot greater, because,
like I say, these guys come in once a month and you don't see them again.
They just set up these guidelines and poof, you know, and they don't care
whether you breach or not. And here's a system that cares.[149]

He noted the feeling of estrangement between local community members
and representatives of the prevailing justice system, such as judges and
probation officers, who only appeared in town on court day. He also expressed faith in the ability of local community members to support and
supervise offenders.[150]

Greg Bragstad believed circle sentencing had affected Sandy Bay and
specific offenders by facilitating a sense of ownership in justice matters among
local residents and by deterring people from committing offences.[151] Sandy
Bay resident Ina Ray expressed a desire for more local community input
into the justice system because of the number of young offenders being
sentenced to jail and the lack of help available to these youths while they
were in custody. She stated:

Yeah, well, it sounds so final, you know, sentence, I can almost hear the jail
door slamming behind them and locked up. As much as I know about the
people in jail, they don't really get any help at all, they're just kind of locked
up and you pay your dues and then you come back, and a lot of the young
people going into jails in Sandy Bay or wherever, especially Aboriginal youth,
they're very troubled and that's why they get in trouble in the first place.
They have a lot of things on their minds. They don't know how to cope with
them, and they see getting into trouble as a way of getting attention or, yeah,
getting the attention they need.[152]

Judge Fafard believed that the criminal justice system suffered from
a lack of credibility in northern Aboriginal communities. He hoped the
sentencing initiatives would improve this situation:

[T]he whole problem with our criminal justice system is that we don't have
credibility at the ground level. That's where we have to build it first, but at
the same time we have to have eyes behind our heads, because we have to
see to it that those people who can exercise some influence and power over
us, such as the Court of Appeal, such as the Ministry of Justice, don't inter-
vene with us too much or at all possibly, while we're doing this business,
while we're building this credibility. I still base myself on the premise that
any system of justice that doesn't have credibility is useless, or practically.
But if you have it, you can't go wrong.[153]

When he introduced circle sentencing to Sandy Bay, Judge Fafard developed criteria to control the selection of cases for this process,[154] with the expectation that the range of cases handled by circle sentencing would expand over time:

> I don't know if those criteria will always be useful or if we'll always stick with them. Certainly I think they will change. But at the beginning while we're gaining experience, we've found they're useful. They've kept us from getting into difficulties that will erode credibility or prevent us from building up credibility. I suppose I shouldn't say erode because I don't know that we have very much yet. We're trying to build a bank of it. . . . Then once we've got a bank of credibility. We can start taking some risks, more risks, we can start doing things that we're afraid to do now.[155]

As of the summer of 1995, only one of his sentencing circle cases had been appealed.[156] He explained why he thought this was the case:

> [The lack of appeals is] probably . . . because of, I suspect, our criteria. We can more or less tell by assessing the case before it goes into a sentencing circle and the potential of rehabilitation of the offender that presents itself on the brief summary that's given to us whether or not it's the kind of case that any court could take a calculated risk [on]. It may be outside the [Court of Appeal] range, but the Court of Appeal itself goes outside the range sometimes to take a calculated risk, and I guess that's what's happening. If the sentencing circle and the motivation of the offender can bring up enough factors, enough resources, and enough potential for rehabilitation . . . the sentencing circle or a judge can say, well, this may not be the norm, this may not fit into the precedent quite exactly, but it's a good case for a calculated risk. So I think that's what we're doing. We're taking, through the sentencing circle, a calculated risk more often than a judge alone would, I think, because we have better information and better motivation on the part of the offender.[157]

Despite his recognition of the judge's power and duty to pronounce sentence within Canadian criminal law, Judge Fafard said he had always followed the consensus developed by circle participants.[158]

The possibility exists that a sentencing circle could be subject to local political pressures. This, as Judge Fafard noted, would damage community perceptions of fairness. One criterion he adopted was the voluntary participation of non-political or non-elected community leaders and elders. At the Northern Justice Society Conference held in June 1993 in Kenora, Ontario, he raised this point and suggested that the credibility of circle sentencing would likely be harmed if the circle became dominated by a local political elite.

In October 1994, Judge Fafard began directing cases to a local sentence advisory committee in Sandy Bay. This committee was to discuss these cases at hearings or circles outside of court. Although the goal was decentralization of the hearing process, he believed a judge should be present from time to time to guard against power imbalances between circle participants:

> At the beginning, until people in the community have some experience with sentencing circles and understand the issues and the pitfalls, I think it's probably important to have some objective outsider there to monitor these things and guard against the pitfalls. But I'm confident that, over time, as people get experience in the sentencing circle and [understand] the purpose of it and problems that can occur if you have an imbalance of power, I think that then people will see to it themselves. . . . But I still think it's a good idea from time to time to select a case in which a judge will be present because I think it gives you an opportunity to monitor the dynamics of the circle [to see] if something is going awry or if a certain person or group of persons in that circle is exercising some unwarranted amount of power over other people. . . . I think if you sit periodically in one of the circles they're having in the community, you can sort of tell what's going on. . . . [for example,] if there are some personality conflicts or if you have a group of people sort of banding together to take over control.[159]

Judge Fafard viewed circle sentencing as complementary to mediation/diversion programs such as the one functioning at Cumberland House. Similarly, Judge Huculak, who is now presiding in Saskatoon but who used to preside in La Ronge and in Sandy Bay from time to time, stressed the importance of developing a mediation/diversion programs in addition to circle sentencing.[160]

Lawyer Sid Robinson commented on the reduced number of sentencing circles occurring at northern court points in 1995. He thought this was due both to fewer requests from offenders and to declining judicial interest in the circles. He felt the amount of court time consumed by sentencing circles was a factor limiting their development. He also suggested that the development of mediation/diversion programs might reduce the number of charges in court and thereby allow more time for sentencing circles. He said sentence advisory committees such as those developed in Sandy Bay and Pelican Narrows would facilitate a circle format while relieving time pressures on the court. Lack of funding for the participants in circle sentencing is also a limiting factor, in his view. Sentencing circles in such locations as Sandy Bay have been supported and co-ordinated by community volunteers who are heavily involved in a multitude of community activities. In his view, a salaried infrastructure is required to support circle sentencing, but he sensed a reluctance on the part of government officials to consider such funding.[161]

At the time of this study, RCMP constable Brian Brennan had been stationed in Sandy Bay since June 1993. He was involved in several sentencing circles, and he expressed concern over the lack of organization and structure in circle sentencing. He was in favour of community sentencing recommendations developed in the absence of the judge to conserve court time:

> I think sentencing circles could be an excellent pre-court, post-charge appearance method of dealing with a lot of cases . . . especially with the youth . . . if it was in the power of the police to say, well, we believe this should go before a sentencing circle, if the person's willing to accept that. And then they would go before a sentencing circle before the person makes a plea in court and . . . the sentencing circle would make the recommendation to the judge that this person should receive whatever sentence they believe. Person goes to court, basically reconfirms his guilty plea in front of the judge, judge will accept the sentencing circle, and you wouldn't tie up the courts with a lot of trials and adjournments and what-not. Because up here we do court once a month, and every second month is a docket day, and every second month after that is a trial day.[162]

He recognized the deterrent effect of sentencing circles upon offenders and suggested this process might be effective in achieving reconciliation between offender, victim, and community:

> [W]hen the sentencing circle is actually taking place, you actually see a lot of things come out that may not be relevant to the exact charge, but there's other emotions and things that have been brewing for a long time. And it seems that once these people have got this out in the open, we don't really have any problem again between those two people.[163]

He illustrated this point by describing a sentencing circle held for a young offender charged with assaulting another youth. During the circle it became apparent that this assault was only one symptom of a long-standing dispute between two families. After a full airing of this dispute, a form of reconciliation between families was achieved. The police did not have problems with the offender or either family after the circle.

Diane Christianson was the probation officer for Sandy Bay at the time of this study.[164] Stationed in Creighton, Saskatchewan, she had covered this court point since April 1993 and had had little involvement with circle sentencing other than the preparation of pre-sentence reports for cases in which an offender had asked for a circle.[165] She believed circle sentencing had empowered Sandy Bay community members and had resulted in a greater sense of offender accountability to community and family.

6 | The Elders' or Community Sentencing Panel

Direct consultation with community members at sentencing was advocated by the Law Reform Commission of Canada in 1974. The commission suggested allowing local community members to sit with the judge and to "assist in the disposition and sentence." This was said to be a long-standing practice in countries such as Denmark.[1] In 1991, the commission developed this theme in an Aboriginal context:

> [L]ay assessors (elders or other respected members of the community) ought to be permitted by express statutory provision to sit with a judge to advise on appropriate sentences. . . . Their duties would include consulting those involved and recommending an appropriate disposition to the judge. Similar programs already exist or are being created in some communities. The advisors' recommendations may differ from the range of sentences established by case law, or may be contrary to general court of appeal jurisprudence. We see no real difficulty in this; indeed, it is because such guidelines are on occasion inappropriate to Aboriginal communities that we make this recommendation.[2]

There clearly is no legal impediment to community consultation during sentencing.

Rupert Ross described the role of elders in the sentencing process at the Sandy Lake Reserve in northwestern Ontario:

> [W]e place a long trestle tables in such a way that they form a large square. The judge, his clerk and his reporter occupy one side of the square. To his right are [three] Elders and an interpreter. Directly across from the judge is where the defense lawyers, offenders and their families sit, together with probation officers and others who may wish to address the court. The fourth part of the square is occupied by the Crown Attorney and those police officers involved in the cases at hand. . . . If a conviction is entered, the next question is the sentence thought to be most appropriate. It is at this point that the Elders have an opportunity to speak to the accused and family members, and to make recommendations about the sentence they believe will be most productive from a community perspective. The Elders bring to the court their knowledge of the accused and his or her family circumstances, and their appreciation of the specific events that might have contributed to the commission of the offence.[3]

An approach similar to the elders' sentencing panel is being used in some Yukon communities. Chief Judge Lilles in *J.A.P.*,[4] stated that one of the submissions he considered in arriving at an appropriate sentence included "evidence and representations by Chief David Keenan, Chief of Teslin Tlingits, representing the five clan leaders, the Tlingit Council and the community recommending a community-based disposition instead of incarceration."[5]

The sentencing practices I observed at Pukatawagan, Manitoba, were similar to the elders' panel, although not all the members of the local justice committee were elders.[6] Judges sitting in Pukatawagan court consulted directly with committee members. Judge William Martin of The Pas described the evolution of community participation in sentencing at the Provincial Court at Pukatawagan:

> It was about six years ago that the chief of the Pukatawagan Band started an initiative, I think assisted by Joyce Dalmyn, to institute and get rolling a type of justice committee at Pukatawagan and to explore the possibilities of having the court function with more input from the community itself. Initially, there were five, possibly six, members of that justice committee—and I speak now of 1989/1990—and we held some very moving and, to my mind, very fruitful sentencing meetings with the whole of the community present.[7]

Initially members of the justice committee sat with other community members in the body of the court when they were advising on sentence; later they sat beside the judge. Lawyer Joyce Dalmyn described this evolution:

> [F]or about the past . . . two years, rather than having rows of chairs in the audience, we have the chair[s] set up so that there's a large circle formed, or sometimes a double circle, depending on how many people are present, because [on] docket days often there are sixty or eighty people on a docket, so the circle sometimes is quite large. So the justice committee used to sit among the members of the public and then some members of the justice committee felt that they should be sitting somewhere else. . . . [W]e've had a couple of different meetings between the entire court party and justice committee members and members of the RCMP. So there's been sort of this evolution, but now, as a whole, they tend to sit at the front with the judge.[8]

Joyce Dalmyn also described one memorable consultation between the presiding judge and the justice committee:

> The judge said that he viewed any sexual assault to be serious. . . . [T]hen he stated to the justice committee, "I feel that in this case jail is appropriate,

but I want you to tell me whether you think I should give him a really high fine, around $1,000, or whether I should send him to jail." And then he conducted a poll or a vote and the justice committee voted and decided that this man should get a $1,000 fine in addition to probation terms—which is what the justice committee had basically recommended to the judge because the offender had already indicated he would go to a lengthy alcohol treatment program, and he had a number of things going in his favour, including being accepted for university. . . . So I've never seen anything quite that particular but, based on the vote, the justice committee prevailed and he got a $1,000 fine in addition to probation![9]

The process followed at Pukatawagan provided more information to the court about both offender and offence than was usually available through counsel. Judges here also consulted justice committee members to verify defence counsel claims about offender rehabilitation. This approach, while allowing the court access to more information, may impede attempts at reconciliation among the offender, victim, and community by stressing the role of justice committee members as witnesses of offender behaviour rather than as resources for the healing and support of the offender.

Although the practices of community sentencing consultation in court vary between jurisdictions, judges, and courts, all approaches bestow a distinct status upon elders or other community representatives within the sentencing process. When elders were acting in an advisory capacity to the court, I found that they assumed a quasi-judicial role similar to that of the lay assessor in Britain.[10]

It is not easy to fully understand the empowering effect on lay people of allowing their participation in a process that was previously off limits. When I attended a sentencing circle at the Red Earth Cree Nation on October 10, 1997,[11] I was struck by the expressions of emotion on the faces of all elders and community members present. For most, this was the first time they had been asked to state their opinions in court. Most speakers were passionate and provided well-thought-out suggestions, in Cree, on how the offender could be helped to change his behaviour. At the end of the circle, all present appeared to believe that they had contributed in a positive way to the sentence pronounced.

In analysing elder and community involvement in sentencing, Judge Brian Giesbrecht, an associate chief judge of the Provincial Court of Manitoba in Brandon, commented on the significant number of initiatives that had been commenced and abandoned in Aboriginal communities in Manitoba and Ontario over the past twenty years. He noted an elders' panel set up by Judge Kopstein at the Rousseau River Reserve in Manitoba, which had functioned for some time before falling apart. Judge Kopstein described an elders' sentencing panel he had used at Rousseau River in the mid-1970s:

two elders, appointed by the chief, had sat with him during court and had advised him on appropriate sentence.[12] Judge Giesbrecht's analysis pointed to the difficulty of keeping the community, and perhaps the judges and lawyers, interested and involved in community sentencing. He believed these projects failed for a variety of reasons, including changes in local leadership, the loss of government funding, or the departure of a key person involved in the initiative, usually a judge or an influential member of the community.

The Elders Justice Advisory Council at Waywayseecappo, Manitoba

An elders' sentencing panel was introduced in 1994 at court in Waywayseecappo, Manitoba. The Elders Justice Advisory Council sat with the judge in court and provided advice during sentencing. Court was conducted in a circle format with other participants, including police, defence and Crown counsel, and the local probation officer. The elders provided the judge with information on each offender and with advice on sentence.

Community Overview

Waywayseecappo is located 351 kilometres (218 miles) northwest of Winnipeg. The reserve encompasses just over one township (10,060 hectares/24,856 acres) of rolling land. The community's economic base is agriculture. On-reserve facilities include a K-12 school, a health office, a band office, recreation facilities, a community centre, and an arena complex. This band is a signatory to Treaty 4, signed in 1874. It has approximately fifteen hundred members, with two-thirds of the band residing on the reserve.[13] The band's native language is Ojibway.[14]

Sergeant Roy of the RCMP detachment at Rossburn[15] indicated Waywayseecappo had grown in population substantially since the late 1980s during a program of housing construction. He sensed the recent development of a middle class on the reserve as a result of increased on-reserve employment opportunities through such projects as the Waywayseecappo school. Prior to December 1993, the Provincial Court had sat only in Rossburn, approximately 15 kilometres (9 miles) from Waywayseecappo. At the time of this study, monthly court hearings were being held on the reserve in a local community hall across from the band office.[16] Later, court was moved to the Waywayseecappo Arena Complex.

Introduction and Development of the Elders Justice Advisory Council

The Provincial Court at Waywayseecappo is conducted in a circle format. The hearings include only docket court and sentencing of offenders from the local community. Trials and preliminary hearings continue to be held in

Rossburn. The Elders Justice Advisory Council is made up of elders from the Waywayseecappo First Nation; the council sit in the circle with the judge, police, the local probation officer, and defence and Crown counsel.[17]

The sentencing initiative at Waywayseecappo grew out of consultations between Associate Chief Judge Giesbrecht and local community representatives.[18] A justice proposal was submitted to the provincial government by the community in 1994. The chief and council of Waywayseecappo asked for court to be moved from Rossburn to the reserve as 95 percent of the cases being heard in Rossburn originated in Waywayseecappo; Judge Giesbrecht agreed. In response to the justice proposal, the provincial government provided funding for the hall rental for court, the establishment of a resident probation officer, and a per diem allocation for elders sitting on the elders' council.[19] Community consultation determined that the model to be used in court would be the elders' council.[20] In addition to sitting with the judge and court on scheduled court days,[21] the elders' council held meetings a week before and a week after monthly court dates. Offenders and accused appearing in court were either ordered or encouraged by the court, with support from the elders, to attend these meetings, which featured traditional Ojibway lessons, talking circles, healing circles, sweet grass ceremonies, smudging, and traditional prayers.[22]

When I visited Waywayseecappo on March 2, 1995, court was held in a rectangular room. The front half contained a circle of chairs for the court party, with microphones in the centre to record proceedings. The back half contained rows of chairs set up in conventional courtroom fashion. Associate Chief Judge Giesbrecht expressed some concern to me that the room was not the ideal shape to accommodate a circle-type of court as the participants seated in the back half of the room were essentially relegated to the role of audience. This appeared to be the case, as the accused called forward appeared not to know whether they should sit with the court party in the circle or stand during consideration of their charges. The circle included Judge Giesbrecht, three elders, Sergeant Roy, local probation officer Herman Mentuck, defence counsel Merv Hart and Bob Harrison, and Crown attorney Lawrence McInnes. Court opened and closed with an Ojibway prayer offered by an elder who wore ceremonial dress and held an eagle feather in her hand. Proceedings included a combination of docket (arraignments and pleas or elections) and sentencings carried over from earlier court dates or other court locations. The elders, who sat on both sides of the judge, participated only in sentencing.

During sentencing, Crown and defence counsel made submissions on offences and offender circumstances and on appropriate sentence. Associate Chief Judge Giesbrecht then asked the elders to comment. They provided information about each offender, stated their opinions of his or her needs, and made recommendations on appropriate sentence. No victims appeared in the court circle and no offenders personally addressed the court. One young offender was asked by Judge Giesbrecht if he understood the terms of his probation order and that court was being adjourned to June on his outstanding charge. He said he understood.

The elders generally voiced a perspective opposing jail. When I interviewed Crown attorney Lawrence McInnes after court, he noted that the elders rarely, if ever, suggested jail for an individual, but they did distinguish between cases in the forcefulness of their submissions against jail. Indeed, on the day I attended the court, the elders forcefully argued against jail for a young offender charged with a break and enter in Rossburn. Associate Chief Judge Giesbrecht accepted the recommendation and placed the young person on strict probation, despite the Crown's request for closed-custody disposition. However, when it came to the case of an adult offender charged with breach of recognizance by drinking and contacting his spouse (whom he was also charged with assaulting), the elders, while not advocating jail, were less vocal in their defence. Apparently, this offender had been asked to attend the elders' council meeting back in January, when his charge had been adjourned, and he had only recently done so. Judge Giesbrecht sentenced the man to seventy-five days in jail.

Perspectives of Community Members and Justice System Personnel on Developments at Waywayseecappo

I interviewed members of the elders' council after court. One stressed her role as a traditional Ojibway healer; all acknowledged the importance of traditional Ojibway spirituality to their work. The elders clearly believed their council was having a positive effect, although they did not further evaluate its impact. Crown attorney Lawrence McInnes later told me that all the elders currently sitting on the council abstained from the consumption of alcohol. He said one of them viewed former Prime Minister John Diefenbaker as a great enemy of their people because his human rights initiatives had lead to the removal of the prohibition of alcohol on reserves. Sergeant Roy stressed that the elders chosen by the chief and council for the elders' council were highly respected at Waywayseecappo. By contrast, both Sergeant Roy and McInnes indicated that some other elders on the reserve did not enjoy such community respect and noted that one had been in custody on March 2, 1995, and had been remanded in custody for a later appearance in court at Brandon.

I also interviewed Herman Mentuck, the local probation officer and a member of the community. Mentuck's job included supervision of offenders on court-ordered probation and undertakings, and the preparation of pre-sentence reports for adults and youth. He regretted he had not had the time to focus on community education through meetings and workshops. Although he was unable to make a final judgement on the impact of the elders' council, as it had only been in operation for a short time, he thought offenders felt more comfortable appearing before their elders at Waywayseecappo than before the conventional court in Rossburn. He viewed the elders' council as a starting point for local community involvement in the justice system and as a way to incorporate traditional Ojibway teaching and practices into court procedure. He predicted the impact of the elders' council would not be seen for some time as many local people were still unaware of it. However, the sentencing initiative, in his view, had served as a form of community empowerment for Waywayseecappo and as a means for his people to achieve a stronger sense of their own identity. Overall, he believed the elders' council had given some offenders a chance to stabilize their lives through use of traditional Ojibway practices. Mentuck was not prepared to generalize from the experience at Waywayseecappo to other communities. He stressed that all communities are different and noted his belief that local community interest in re-establishing the prominence of traditional Ojibway teachings and practices had facilitated the initiative. He believed communities in which Christianity was strong were less likely to accept the type of re-integration of traditional practices seen at Waywayseecappo.[23]

Associate Chief Judge Giesbrecht had attended court at Waywayseecappo on a number of occasions since introduction of the elders' council. He was supportive of the elders' council initiative and hoped it would facilitate more local involvement in justice matters. He recognized that previously outsiders had performed all functions within the justice system for the people of Waywayseecappo. While stressing local community responsibility for choosing the elders' council model as a vehicle for local participation, he noted health problems among elders on the council as a problem that was affecting development of the sentencing initiative. As of March 1995, of the five elders on the panel, two were unable to participate as one had cancer and the other had high blood pressure. He also questioned the degree of respect accorded these elders by younger people in the community.[24]

I interviewed Crown attorney Lawrence McInnes and RCMP sergeant Roy after court on March 2, 1995. Both viewed the elders' council as a positive step for the community and as a vehicle for local community empowerment. Overall, McInnes observed significant progress by the Waywayseecappo community. He commented that twenty years ago the reserve had been an extremely violent place with a significant number of murders. He felt the situation had improved greatly. Both Sergeant Roy and McInnes acknowledged the respect accorded the elders on the council by local community members and felt these elders offered valuable insights to assist sentencing deliberations. Sergeant Roy indicated the difficulty, at such an early stage, of interpreting the impact of the elders' council. He reported no change in recent RCMP case statistics from Waywayseecappo, although the local population had increased steadily in recent years. Both men viewed the role of local probation officer Herman Mentuck as indispensable to the success of the council.

Defence lawyer Merv Hart, who was employed by Manitoba Legal Aid in Brandon, had appeared regularly in Waywayseecappo court since the introduction of the elders' council. He thought that the elders' focus was on offender rehabilitation rather than on retribution and that the elders were decent people who were attempting to help local offenders. He recalled the elders being very stern when addressing several young offenders who had broken into the local school, and he suggested that the embarrassment of appearing before the council had likely served as a deterrent to these youths.[25]

7 | The Sentence Advisory Committee

In *Rich,*[1] Justice O'Regan of the Newfoundland Supreme Court (Trial Division) commented that information available through a sentencing circle involving a judge could also be obtained by "hearing the results of the consensus of the community from their own sentencing circle with the accused and without the complainant and the judge."[2] At the time of my study, this practice was being employed at Cumberland House, Sandy Bay, and Pelican Narrows, Saskatchewan, where presiding judges seeking a recommendation on sentence referred cases to a local sentence advisory committee. This committee, described by participants as the "sentencing circle committee" in all three locations, met with offenders (and sometimes with victims) before reaching a recommendation.

Community participation in the sentencing of young offenders at Sandy Bay began in 1989. Judge Fafard described the formation and functioning of a sentencing advisory committee for young offenders in that community:

> The idea for a sentencing advisory committee came from my efforts to create a mechanism to get some community input. As a provincial court judge, I don't sit with a jury. I have no authority under the *Criminal Code* to have a jury of people with me to decide the facts. However, I can get advice from the community after the verdict has been reached in a case. If a person is found guilty, many opportunities to consult with the community are available. . . . In putting together the pre-sentence report, for example, the probation officer will go out and speak to those involved in the case, the victim, and to the relatives of the offender. However, the pre-sentence report doesn't give you the wisdom of the Elders and others who live in the community—those who may know the offender and the victim—but who are not directly involved in the case. So there was a need for some mechanism to involve them. . . . I began in Sandy Bay because I have some close friends there. We had coffee during an adjournment and we discussed the possibilities. I discussed the ideas with another provincial court judge and he was very favourable. I then planted the idea with the community that, if they wanted to have input into the court process, they should identify people to be on a sentencing advisory committee.[3]

Harry Morin, a committee member, described the procedure:

The first thing that happened was the magistrate [judge] designated the young offenders to us, and he would say . . . , "I expect your recommendations at the next court date." So, normally, court is once a month so we had a month to work on it. . . . [Then] we had consent forms made. . . . After that was done, then we'd set a meeting date with the young offender. Normally we held ours at the village office at the council chambers, where it was more private and after hours nobody would bother us. We'd sit down with the young offender and start questioning the young offender—what he's done, what had happened. And we try looking at why was he doing these things.[4]

Committee member Ina Ray felt her committee positively influenced young offenders by opening lines of communication with them:

I don't think any of those young people, well maybe one or two, have repeated or got into trouble again with the law. . . . But more important than that, I think, is the whole rapport that I think we set up with these young people, just making connection with them as an adult and as the older people that were on this committee. It's not very often that we have the opportunity to reach out and to talk to our young people. You know in this busy world they look after their interests, we look after ours, and yet we're all living in this community together, and yet we don't have that chance to sort of talk between generations.[5]

At Pelican Narrows, Judge Fafard began referring cases to the local sentence advisory committee in the spring of 1994. The Peter Ballantyne Band actively supported community participation by appointing members to this committee.[6] Committee co-ordinator Derek Custer described this advisory process:

Yes, in most cases the judge prefers that we talk with the accused as well as the victim prior to . . . the court date. So what I do is I gather up the committee people and we sit down with the accused as well as the victim, if he or she is willing to sit down with us, and then we make recommendations. Now once this happens, we write down the recommendations, type them up, and then I approach the judge. And during that date of the court, I give the recommendations to the judge. He looks at them and approves them. Once they're approved then the accused will have to follow what we recommended.[7]

He explained the specific procedure followed when meeting with offenders:

We meet at a certain date, maybe a couple days before the court date, or a week, depending on who's available in the committee. . . . [W]e start out with a prayer and then everything is read aloud to the committee, what the offence is, and as well we ask the offender if he really fully understands the reasoning for the sentencing circle. Some do and some don't. But during our meeting, when we get together, we explain to the offender what happens in the circle. See this is their opportunity to turn their lives around instead of getting into trouble all the time. This is the time to, you know, reflect back on what's happened to their lives and people are caring and they're trying to help. And we explain this to every offender that comes to the circle, and then we proceed to give proper recommendations for that offender, and to follow through, and as well make sure they agree with what we've recommended. [We check] if they're willing to do it. And once they agree, then everything is typed up, the recommendations, and then the judge will look at them.[8]

The sentence advisory process was in its infancy in the Saskatchewan communities I studied. Despite his warning that "it may be too early" to draw any conclusions from the community sentencing initiatives,[9] Judge Fafard professed his belief in the effectiveness of the process as a deterrent:

[Y]ou could say that in Pelican Narrows, . . . because our case load there diminished fairly dramatically since we've started doing sentencing circles, maybe you could conclude from that that it's having an impact on actual crime. Because it may be, . . . if people believe that the system of administration of justice that supervises them . . . is functioning for them and by them in their own best interests, that they're less likely to go against it.[10]

According to Judge Fafard, the advisory committee at Pelican Narrows tended to be more demanding, and stricter in its recommendations respecting probation orders, than he himself would have been.[11] It was also clear that this local advisory committee was unaccustomed to being given this level of input into the system and that they were struggling to achieve their own understanding of what an appropriate disposition or sentence would entail. Recognition that community decision making, as it relates to local perceptions of punishment, is a new skill to be learned was reflected in the following comments from Judge Fafard:

I think that to a large extent people haven't made up their minds about this, well, because they've never been called upon to think about it. We've done all the thinking and dictating, and now we're asking people to make decisions. We're presenting them the opportunity to think about it and the motivation to give it some thought. They're motivated to think about it because they have some responsibility to decide, you know, so now people really have to seriously address their minds to it.[12]

It is clear that debate over such key issues as punishment will continue. As local communities are given further input into and control within the formal justice system, it is unavoidable that their understanding of these issues and their ability to articulate local viewpoints to the court will be enhanced.

The sentencing circle committee at Cumberland House served as a sentence advisory committee and also handled cases of mediation/diversion. When I made a field trip to Cumberland House on December 12, 1994, two cases were considered by the committee in its sentence advisory capacity. In each case, the committee met with the offenders and attempted to reach a consensus on a sentence recommendation. One case in particular displayed the internal workings of such a committee. It involved an eighteen-year-old offender charged with assault.

Before the offender entered the meeting room, the committee considered the details of the assault provided by the police and developed a tentative recommendation. The offender had been drunk and had assaulted a friend at a party. As the offender had no criminal record, the police had recommended a suspended sentence with probation. The committee decided on a one-year probation order requiring her to abstain from alcohol consumption. They also wanted her to take alcohol counseling and to apologize to the victim. The offender did not agree. She emphasized that her friend had received only six months' probation for a similar offence. A struggle ensued as the committee attempted to convince the offender that she should agree with the recommendation, while the offender tried to convince the committee to reduce the recommended probationary period to six months. Eventually, the committee members came to the unanimous conclusion that the offender could either agree with their recommendation or have the charge referred back to the court without recommendation (in which case the offender could "take her chances with the judge"). The offender then agreed with the recommendation, and the matter was finalized pending appearance before the judge on the next court date.

It is too early to draw conclusions about the overall impact of the sentence advisory process; however, it appears to have alleviated time pressures on the court—in contrast to lengthy sentencing circles—while at the same time facilitating community sentencing input. Although the time saved for the court party may be viewed as a benefit, arguably the most telling lesson to be taken from the development of sentence advisory committees is the significant role that local community members can play without direct supervision by the court. This lay involvement may enhance feelings of community ownership of the process, while at the same time providing additional resources to the court.

The Sentence Advisory Process
at Pelican Narrows, Saskatchewan
Community Overview

Pelican Narrows is located 100 kilometres (62 miles) northwest of Flin Flon, Manitoba, on a 530-hectare (1,304-acre) reserve inhabited by the Peter Ballantyne Band. This band signed Treaty 6 in 1889 as part of the Lac La Ronge Band. The native language at Pelican Narrows is Cree. Its population is 2,200.[13] Local services included an elementary school and a high school, a variety store, a post office, the Peter Ballantyne Band offices, an alcohol treatment centre, a health centre, and a seven-member RCMP detachment. In recent years, the Peter Ballantyne Band has been divided by a land settlement reached between the chief and council and the federal government. A dissident group within the band had tried, unsuccessfully, to prevent execution of the agreement. At the time of this study, court was being held three days a month at Pelican Narrows. The court party flew in from La Ronge and probation services were provided by road from Creighton.

Introduction and Development
of the Sentence Advisory Process

In 1994, Judge Fafard began referring cases to a local committee in Pelican Narrows, asking for a community recommendation on sentence. This committee, called the "sentencing circle committee" by its members, had been organized by the chief and council of the Peter Ballantyne Band. Cases were considered in the presence of victims and offenders. Proceedings, conducted in Cree, developed sentence recommendations that were later presented at court. Judge Fafard described the process:

> The band has appointed people to be responsible to see that this portfolio stays on the move. So the interest is always there. I can easily refer cases to a sentencing circle in Pelican Narrows. A lot of those cases I don't attend myself. I just refer the case to the sentencing circle. They get together, they have their circle, and then they give me written recommendations. And that seems to be working fairly well.[14]

Co-ordinator Derek Custer said the committee met with offenders and victims (if they were willing) and reached recommendations on sentence. He emphasized the committee's desire to have victims present:

When we started off, we thought the victims would be there but . . . [during our first circles] the victim wasn't there. So we had to go without the victim. Just recently the victims of each crime have started to show up within the circle. And that is good for the circle. . . . There's an understanding between the victim and offender that the victim is . . . given an apology from the offender, and the reason for that is . . . we want to keep a healthy environment within the community so there's no revenge taken from the victim towards the offender. We . . . want to make him understand that. So that is why we recommend that the victim will be in the circle too.[15]

Derek Custer also identified the committee's role in supervising offenders:

The rest of the committee, they supervise as well . . . because . . . one person can't really supervise so many clients. . . . So, therefore, the person that's in trouble with the law, he is very cautious because there's a lot of people keeping an eye on him. . . . So that's how it works. Not only one person, but a committee itself and there . . . are more people getting involved, then the better it works for us. The recommendations will be followed.[16]

This supervisory role was emphasized by RCMP corporal Bob MacMillan:

[B]ecause these [offenders are] before a sentencing circle or healing circle, they know who was in the healing circle, and so it's almost like having another extra eight sets of eyes out there because these people know each one of these eight persons was there, know what's happened, know what the recommendations were. So, if the recommendations were not to drink, well, then you have got to be careful. And then the word's going to get back, and there's a lot of community pressure. . . . If you go to jail from a white judge, nobody cares. Oh well. However, if the community gets on your case, then it's a different story, because now you've got different people of the community, maybe the heads of different families, and they're going to tell their family and everybody will know that he was at a sentencing circle, and Joe Blow got six months' probation with no drinking. Well, now there's a whole bunch of people that know that he shouldn't be drinking, and they apply pressure. So I think in a lot of ways it should work.[17]

Derek Custer explained that his committee had also developed a rule forbidding subsequent appearances before the committee. The rule served as an inducement for offenders to take advantage of this one opportunity by making positive changes in their lives consistent with the committee's conditions. The sentencing circle committee at Pelican Narrows also played a role in sentencing circles that were conducted in court with a judge.

Perspectives of Community Members and
Justice System Personnel on Developments at Pelican Narrows

Co-ordinator Derek Custer stressed the need for community education about his committee to expand its effectiveness:

> The circle was questioned at first. But I think people are starting to realize what's going on. You know, people are starting to have interest in it. I think they're starting to realize that it's benefitting the criminals within the community. Instead of going to jail, they'd prefer to stay here and that's one of the objectives within the circle that we have. We'd rather have the offender stay within the community instead of going out to jail, because [it] just brings resentment when people go out to jail. So when we keep them in the community, they're starting to realize that there's caring people in the community, they want to do something good for them.[18]

Committee member Cecile Merasty[19] noted that most people were scared to serve on the committee as they feared offender reaction, but she felt community education would facilitate greater participation. Merasty also believed most offenders appearing in Provincial Court did not understand the procedure or language used by the judge and therefore remained mute. However, during circles conducted in Cree by the sentencing circle committee, offenders were empowered to explain why they had committed offences and what steps they were prepared to take to correct such wrongs. She commented on the counter-productivity of sending local offenders to jail, which resulted in a further build-up of anger and retaliatory behaviour upon their return to Pelican Narrows. Both Derek Custer and Cecile Merasty acknowledged jail had its place for serious crimes but felt minor property damage and assaults should be dealt with locally through community-based sentences.

Community members speaking at the Pelican Narrows circle stressed that their committee's work would provide an opportunity for community empowerment as long as offenders recognized their wrongdoing and agreed to change their behaviour. Although recognizing the importance of community participation in the committee's work, one elder viewed further outside resources as necessary to continued development of circle sentencing in Pelican Narrows. Another elder maintained that the local community had a greater impact on offenders than outsiders such as the court party.

Judge Fafard questioned whether the justice system could be in any way effective in a community without local participation, and he suggested the community's "face" might be better than that of an external system. He believed the justice system worked best when a community believed in it and had faith in it.[20] When I interviewed him in November of 1994, he said he was impressed with the efforts the Pelican Narrows community had made through its sentencing circle committee and said that if he had been asked a year and a half earlier, he would not have believed or predicted such a degree of involvement.[21] Despite the early stage of this initiative, he viewed the committee and the introduction of circle sentencing as having had some impact at Pelican Narrows, as measured by a decrease in the court's case load.[22] Judge Huculak also recognized this community's desire for active participation in the justice system; however, she felt local community members lacked the confidence to expand the reach of their sentencing circle committee into the area of mediation/diversion without outside assistance.[23]

Corporal Bob MacMillan expressed the support of the RCMP for the development of circle sentencing both in court and through the sentence advisory committee. He viewed the development of local mediation as a logical next step and felt local people wanted a greater say in the justice system:

> They recognize the judicial system in the North doesn't fulfil the role it should be fulfilling, and they've wanted a say for quite some time. This is their opportunity to finally have some say. And there's a couple [of] people, some people in the band, that are very gung ho. James Merasty, for one, is pretty much a leader in bringing or changing the justice system to where the people actually will have input into the justice system. So . . . there has been a lot of evolution over the last one and a half years, and things are going to continue to evolve here.[24]

He recognized the failings of the prevailing Canadian justice system in northern Aboriginal communities:

> The judicial system, in my opinion, . . . doesn't work in the North, at all, for these people. . . . [For example,] two people have a fight on Monday. The victim calls us Tuesday. We investigate it. By the time we collect statements and everything else, it's . . . two weeks down the road. In the meantime, these two persons have patched up their problems, are friends again. And then all of a sudden a summons comes in the mail three weeks later from the offence, to the guy that was the accused and then two months later he's going to court for it. In the meantime, the victim is going, "Well, our problem's over. Why are we doing this?" And then the accused goes to jail. So it solves nothing. The victim is mad then because he was put in a position where he had to come testify against a person he didn't want to testify against. The accused is mad because he thinks, "Well, why are the police doing this if this guy's not mad

any more. Then all of a sudden you're sending me to jail too?" So it's not a system that's . . . right for the people here. I mean, when something happens here they have to be handled forthwith, now, because that's where the problem is—now. Two weeks from now, the problem's gone. It doesn't matter any more.[25]

He viewed community opinion as having more impact on offender behaviour than police or court involvement in Pelican Narrows but doubted circle sentencing would work in a larger community, such as Saskatoon, due to lack of community supervision of the offender and lack of awareness of and concern about the offender's actions.

Lawyer Cathy Bohachik was counsel to one offender sentenced at the Pelican Narrows circle. She had also participated in other sentencing circles in the North. Although she had never attended a meeting of the Pelican Narrows sentencing circle committee outside of court, she believed they were well organized and actively involved in the cases referred to them. She questioned the effectiveness of a sentencing circle with multiple offenders as such circles offer less opportunity for feedback from individual offenders. Despite the criteria developed by the La Ronge judges, she felt there was still some confusion about which cases would be deemed acceptable for circle sentencing, and she felt further guidance from the court was required. She hoped circle sentencing would continue as she felt it was a useful tool in combatting recidivism.[26]

Diane Christianson was the provincial government probation officer covering Pelican Narrows. She resided in Creighton, Saskatchewan, 120 kilometres (75 miles) southeast of Pelican Narrows. Although she was not directly involved in circle sentencing, as Probation Services left such matters to the local community, she made recommendations to the court in pre-sentence reports about the appropriateness of community involvement in sentencing. One pre-sentence report she had prepared recommended against a sentencing circle based on objections voiced by the victim. This recommendation was followed by Judge Fafard.

8 | The Community Mediation Committee

No one sentencing model or initiative should be viewed as the optimal, or indeed the only, vessel for facilitating local participation and input in the justice process. The strength of local participation in circle sentencing is evident in the initiatives discussed in this study and in other initiatives across Canada, such as the Kwanlin Dun Circle process in the Yukon[1] and the Blood Tribe Alternative Sentencing Program (Aissimohkl) in Alberta.[2] As these initiatives have, to varying degrees, involved local community members in the full spectrum of planning, organizing, and supervising circle sentencing, the logical extension of this level of local involvement is complete diversion of offenders from the court system through community mediation committees.

Although mediation does not involve the imposition of a criminal sentence, it does provide for the disposition and resolution of criminal actions by adults and youths diverted from the court system. This process is sanctioned for young persons by section 4 of the *Young Offenders Act* and for adults by sections 717–717.4 of the *Criminal Code*. At the time of fieldwork for this study, these *Criminal Code* sections had yet to be proclaimed; however, the Crown still exercised its discretion in diverting both adults and young offenders within the mediation initiatives studied.

As the police have always had the power to decide whether charges are laid in the first place, an informal form of mediation often occurs at the time a complaint is investigated. Corporal Kirke Hopkins of Pelican Narrows advised that the significant discretion available to police officers in laying charges often places them in the position of working out a solution between aggrieved parties.[3] Thus, a decision not to proceed further with a complaint may indicate that the parties have reached some resolution and do not require further intervention of the system.

The goals of mediation are varied. Professor Michael Jackson described the objectives of an Aboriginal mediation program in High Level, Alberta, in 1981 as including (1) short circuiting the law breaking–incarceration cycles of Native offenders; (2) giving Native people a better understanding of the criminal justice system; (3) increasing community participation in and "ownership" of the criminal justice system; and (4) minimizing the penetration of Native people into the criminal justice system.[4] With these objectives in mind, advocates of criminal mediation have suggested local communities are well equipped to achieve resolution of many disputes previously handled by the court system.

In 1975, the Law Reform Commission of Canada discussed the advantages of community participation in mediation:

> The continuing interest in diversion is fed by many sources. There is a growing disappointment with an over-reliance on the criminal law as a means of dealing with a multitude of social problems. At the same time we realize [that] rehabilitation does not provide a full answer to the problem of crime. Increasingly, it has recognized that crime has social roots and sentencing policies must take into account not only the offender but the community and the victim as well. . . . The general peace of the community may be strengthened more through a reconciliation of the offender and victim [than] through their polarization in an adversary trial. . . . Diversion encourages the community to participate in supporting the criminal justice system to the degree that was not always possible under the trial model. Professionals, para-professionals, ex-offenders and ordinary citizens are encouraged to join the delivery of services to the criminal justice system, for the diversion program rests upon a community base.[5]

In an Aboriginal context, Donald McKay, Jr., a Cree from Cumberland House, explained the relationship between the community, victim, and offender within the mediation process:

> We bring these two people face to face and ask them, "Why'd you do it? For what reason?" and then we get them started talking to each other. . . . The accused can say, "Well, how can I pay you back, what can I do for you? . . . Maybe I can work for you if it's 100 hours, right now in winter time, shoveling snow or chopping wood, or any kind of little chores around the house . . . [as a] form of restitution, instead of paying back money all the time?" Sometimes people bust a window or kick a door down or something like that. Well, maybe that person can, you know, put some money in by replacing a window or door and that type of thing. . . . The biggest thing I have with these community circles [is that] we know the people that's been victimized and we also know the people charged, and I just think it's a whole community healing process. We know them better than the court systems.[6]

In addition to promoting reconciliation between the offender and the victim, and compensation for the victim, local mediation committees also focus on changing offender behaviour. Cyril Roy, chairperson of the Cumberland House sentencing circle committee that also functioned as a community mediation committee, told me he believed interaction between his committee and offenders promoted such a change.[7] RCMP constable Murray Bartley of Cumberland House commented on the deterrent effects of the mediation process on offenders but questioned whether victim restitution was always possible:

> [M]any of these offences are so minor, there's really no victim. And to order [monetary] restitution is impossible. I think it's a lot more difficult to face a group of people in your community such as elders, . . . and, if there is a victim, people you've actually victimized, and to have to actually personally apologize to them. [That's harder] than to just receive a fine and walk away in a courtroom.[8]

A further advantage of local mediation is a savings of time and resources for the police. Corporal Bob MacMillan of Pelican Narrows described this benefit:

> If . . . [local mediation] works . . . it will eliminate a lot of our work, because a lot of our work right now is the type of mischief which would be broken windows. . . . Somebody's having a party and somebody asks somebody to leave and they don't want to. They get thrown out of the house and they grab a rock and throw it through the window and they phone us up and we go investigate. Really, what the victim wants is the window to be repaired. Period. But, if it gets into the legal process, it doesn't work that way.[9]

Mediation is the only model of community participation considered in this study that allows local community members the final decision on disposition. Judge Huculak of La Ronge stressed the empowering impact on communities of this final decision-making power.[10]

The breadth of mediation to date has been limited by the range of offences referred to the local community by the police and courts. During the course of fieldwork for this study, diversion referrals were solely at the discretion of the local police, the Crown prosecutor, or the judge. Effective September 3, 1996, the *Criminal Code* was amended to recognize adult alternative-measures programs. Provinces were delegated the responsibility of defining the criteria for such programs, including the classification of offenders and offences that could be diverted.

Constable Murray Bartley of Cumberland House suggested that mediation should be made available only for minor property offences and not for more serious crimes of violence, which he doubted the committee would be able to handle.[11] However, Donald McKay, Jr., felt that his committee could deal with more serious referrals:

I guess I questioned the judge a couple of times on what kind of cases we could deal with. I guess the far more serious cases, say assault and stuff like that, are too serious for us, according to the judge or court system, to deal with. But we've been dealing with, say, breaking and enter, mischief, damage of property, and cases like that. Assault charges, maybe, between two young people, stuff like that we've been dealing with. But far more serious assault charges where a weapon was used, those ones we haven't been able to deal with. . . . . [However], I keep saying this—I've probably said it ten times—but we are the ones that live here in this community. We are the ones that have to live with these people that commit crimes. And I think we as a community should be dealing with them.[12]

Not surprisingly, many community mediation committees are hesitant to consider serious cases in their early stages of operation. Judge Huculak indicated that, during her attempts to establish the mediation/diversion program in Pelican Narrows, she sensed that the local community lacked the confidence to proceed on their own and wanted to start the mediation process with her direct input.[13] It is likely, however, that further experience with this process will increase the confidence of local community members in dealing with more difficult and challenging cases. According to Judge Fafard, speaking in the context of the development of sentencing circles, "It seems that if people have things done for them and long enough, they lose confidence in their own abilities."[14]

The Justice Committee at the
Mathias Colomb Cree Nation, Pukatawagan, Manitoba
Community Overview

Pukatawagan is located 819 kilometres (510 miles) north of Winnipeg, 210 kilometres (130 miles) north of The Pas,[15] and 40 kilometres (25 miles) downriver from Sandy Bay, Saskatchewan. The community is accessible by air (through an airline owned by the Mathias Colomb Band), by rail, and, in winter, by an ice road from The Pas. The Mathias Colomb Band was formed in 1910 after a group separated from the Peter Ballantyne Band of northwest Saskatchewan. In 1994, the band had a total membership of 1,921 and an on-reserve population of 528. Community services include a hotel, restaurant, convenience store, Laundromat, health-care centre, a crisis centre, and a school. At the time of this study, police services were provided by a detachment of the RCMP and through local band constables and a volunteer peacekeeping group, which patrolled regularly and assisted community members in need.[16]

Prior to the establishment of the RCMP detachment and local sittings of the Provincial Court in Pukatawagan, dispute resolution had been handled within the local community. Elder Gabriel Bighetty gave an example:

> The old people in the old days, I think they were doing way better before the white people came to the community. . . . In the years 1930/31, in between there, people that put themselves into trouble in them old days, the chief and the councillors used to have their own court. They didn't have a court every month, every once in a while. If they would have three people that been in trouble themselves, they'd get them three people and they'd put in court to talk to them, and then the chief would give a sentence to George. "Well, George, you've been doing that." . . . So, they'll tell George, "You go and cut three cords of wood. That's your penalty." [17]

Bighetty said that a representative of the chief and council would check to see if the work was done.

In the 1970s, Pukatawagan came to be known as the Dodge City of the North due to its high rate of violent crime. A 1992 *Winnipeg Free Press* story commented on this history and subsequent changes within Pukatawagan:

> In its violent heyday during the 1970's, Pukatawagan . . . was seeing four slayings a year in a population of only 1200. The RCMP believe this may have been the highest per capita homicide rate in North America. But over the past four years only one homicide has occurred on the reserve, the RCMP report.[18]

By 1995, this situation had improved, in part due to the local justice committee. Committee member Hy Colomb described the changes:

> And then we started to talk about . . . the year 1975, when our Pukatawagan community was a bad place. And you must have heard about that. I don't have to ask you because if you didn't hear about it, it is very funny because the rest of the world did. So, I says, we'll try to bring out a community way better than how it was and [show] how it is now.[19]

Recent years have also witnessed a renewed emphasis on traditional Aboriginal practices at Pukatawagan. Healing circles have been used within the community outside the Provincial Court system, and the local crisis centre conducted a family healing workshop during the summer of 1994.[20]

Resistance to the Provincial Court system was apparent at Pukatawagan during the 1980s and that resistance was still in evidence at the time of this study. In the mid-1980s, members of the band became disenchanted with the circuit court that serviced the reserve from Thompson. Under Chief Pascal Bighetty, a band council resolution was passed prohibiting the court party from entering Pukatawagan. Author Geoffrey York described this resistance:

> Bighetty believed the judges were ignoring the wishes of his 1,400 band members, who wanted tougher jail sentences to battle the rising crime rate in Pukatawagan. "Northern courts have become a farce," the chief declared in 1986. As his frustration mounted, Bighetty warned that he might prohibit the provincial judges from entering his community. A senior provincial official scoffed at the threat and accused the Indians of "grandstanding." That was the last straw for Pascal Bighetty. "The ban is on," the chief announced. "Any provincial court judge, official or lawyer who sets foot in our community will be charged with trespassing." The people of Pukatawagan had the legal right to keep outsiders off their reserve, so the monthly court proceedings were shifted to Lynn Lake, the nearest town.[21]

Lawyer Joyce Dalmyn described the changes to the Provincial Court in Pukatawagan resulting from this incident:

> Pukatawagan used to be run out of the Thompson court system and during the time when Pascal Bighetty was chief, there was a problem where the community BCR'd [passed a band resolution banning] the Thompson court party for various reasons which remain somewhat mysterious, but have something to do with the Crown wanting to leave at 4:30 and other such things and never getting through a docket. And at the request of Chief Bighetty, Judge Martin specifically, out of The Pas, was requested to come to Pukatawagan and have court. So the whole system shifted where probation from The Pas had to take over and the court parties started travelling out of The Pas.[22]

During the course of my study, the Provincial Court was being held in a local community hall in Pukatawagan once a month. In the spring of 1997 the Mathias Colomb Band again refused entry to the court party, with the result that charges for residents of Pukatawagan were transferred to the court in The Pas, approximately 210 kilometres (130 miles) away.

Introduction and Development of Community Mediation

The focal point of community participation in sentencing and mediation in Pukatawagan has been the justice committee. Committee member Hy Colomb, a former chief of the First Nation, described the committee's development:

> Pascal Bighetty was the chief that time, in 1983, so he talked to us about having a justice committee here. [At first] we didn't go to the court on the court days. [Then] [w]e brought it up in our meetings [that] we should go to

the court days so we'll know how this guy gets his sentence and then we'll know who was there and how many times this guy had been in the courts off and on. We'll learn something.[23]

Colomb said the justice committee began by meeting with and counselling troubled community members. Later the committee involved the RCMP and the band's chief and council in their deliberations.

Committee member Liz Bear described how the justice committee is organized:

> There are four women and four men and each one is assigned a specific group to deal with when it comes to dealing with the referrals received from the courts or from the RCMP or from any organization that wants to deal with the misbehaviour of an individual because we all have our own little expertise, I guess, our knowledge of these certain groups.[24]

When I visited Pukatawagan in the spring of 1995, a community review of the justice committee had recently been conducted. This review seems to have been triggered by complaints from community members and women's groups that the committee did not have sufficient training and resources to deal with cases of violence and abuse, especially for repeat offenders. Following the review, as a result of these concerns, the committee was able to deal with "minor charges like first-time offenders," but could not deal with sexual abuse or spousal assault charges.[25] By April of 1995, the committee was mediating minor disputes referred to it from the RCMP, the Provincial Court, and community members or agencies. Members were also regularly attending Provincial Court to advise the judge on sentencing for specific offenders.

Corporal Robert Brossart described the process of referral and the range of cases referred to the justice committee:

> A case can go two ways to the justice committee. It's either referred directly from our office after receiving a complaint, or the provincial judge's court will send a matter over to be dealt with by the justice committee. They'll hear the circumstances and they'll set some kind of penalty or some kind of help to work with the person. . . . Now, the charges vary depending on what we send to them, but we have a tendency of sending less serious charges to them because they're still in the developmental stages and still learning court procedures, etc., so they try to work out some of the minor squabbles and minor assaults and things like that that happen within the community.[26]

Liz Bear described how cases were also referred to the justice committee by local community members without the involvement of the formal justice system:

> Like the commonest ones that we have is harassment . . . family feuds or whatever, or there was a misgiving at some time and when the person is perhaps under the influence. They go and verbally harass the person in a public area or they vent out to their kids or stuff like that. We get those referrals made here. . . . We always ask the complainant, "What would you like to see out of this situation? What's your recommendation?" Then I bring that back here and then we talk about it again. Say Mrs. Smith put a complaint against Mrs. Somebody. So I want to ask Mrs. Smith, "What do you want? What would you be comfortable with to [settle] this thing?"[27]

The committee met regularly with offenders, and often with victims, in an effort to resolve disputes. The committee often directed offenders to take corrective action, such as counselling by an elder, alcohol treatment, or making an apology or restitution to the victim. Committee member Hy Colomb gave an example:

> We have our meetings and the guy who makes the trouble comes in, and then our chairperson, Chief Caribou, would tell this guy, "Here," he says, "you go and see George every week for two months." Well, that means this guy has to go and talk to George eight times. Well, George will be talking to this guy and explaining [to] him all kinds of things, how to get him out of trouble. After two months, George had a report in to us that this guy had been to him there every week, eight times. Well, that was his sentence. But that's good.[28]

Committee member Gabriel Bighetty described efforts by the committee to compensate victims monetarily for property damage suffered by deducting costs from the offender's welfare cheque: "So because they can't pay, the only thing to do is just find out what to do now. We go and ask the council and the chief to take out from their welfare so much every month."[29]

Reconciliation between offender and victim was another of the goals of the justice committee, as Liz Bear explained:

> We ask the victim to come in. Either they come in with the offender there—like the two parties involved—or one at a time we hear their side of the story. If the victim or the complainant is comfortable, they can come and listen as to what we're going to say to the perpetrator or whatever you want to call him. . . . That's our intent to always put people back into a relationship . . . relative, wife's family, wives, whatever way. It is to come back and see and to stand corrected that somebody did indeed do a wrong, otherwise that

complaint wouldn't be here. . . . There would be an apology given. There would just be a time that they air out their differences here and we're sitting and we're giving guidance or providing some advice.[30]

To increase compliance with their dispositions, the committee developed a practice of allowing offenders to appear before it only three times, after which the offender would be referred back to the formal court system. Committee member George Colomb explained:

Three times to [the] justice committee. Whether they are going to take their elders' advice or whether he is going to take advice what they are working for. If they don't do it, the next time he comes in on the third time, he doesn't show up or he doesn't want to do it, he wants to play his own game, so we just give him to the [Provincial] Court. So, that's where he cannot speak for himself. He could speak for himself in here but over there is a different world, he couldn't even speak for himself. All he has to do is what the court said. He has to do it, whether he likes it or not.[31]

Despite the generally less serious nature of cases being referred to the committee by the RCMP and the court during my visit to Pukatawagan in the spring of 1995, lawyer Joyce Dalmyn noted that, for an eight-month period in 1993, many spousal assault charges had been referred to the justice committee for mediation, largely because the Crown realized there was little chance of conviction, given the reluctance of the complainants to testify. Corporal Robert Brossart described this form of resistance to the court system:

Spousal assaults, for a while, were going to the justice committee. . . . [The] reason for that . . . is testifying is not really big or high on the priority list. We've received numerous complaints at this detachment. However, when it comes time for the actual trial date, very few trials go ahead due to the fact the complainant no longer wishes to pursue the matter. . . . They find it easier with the justice committee to maybe try and help that problem or assist it as opposed to with the provincial courts. The spouse doesn't want to testify. Therefore, the charge is stayed and nothing is done.[32]

Joyce Dalmyn stated that victims had usually been involved in circle sentencing, and she described concerns about the lack of victim involvement in mediation through the justice committee. She stated:

One of the problems when we initially were diverting matters from court to the justice committee, one of the big problems that happened was, the victims were not being involved. And then the victim would come to court and say,

"Well, this is crap. I don't want anything to do with it. I want this guy to be punished." So then in order for the Crown to allow something, it was stated very specifically in court that the victim had to go to the justice committee meeting.[33]

Corporal Brossart echoed this concern:

> So now they're trying the healing aspect of it, where a lot of times the victim isn't taken into consideration, where the courts show, okay, this victim's been assaulted, this victim has had a broken window. As a result of that, buddy is going to pay a fine or pay you for the damage, or he's raped you [and] he's going to jail for a period of time. Whereas on the other side, the justice committee, well, it's all an alcohol problem—we'll send you to a NADAP worker or to . . . alcohol treatment or anger management treatment.[34]

Despite such concerns, at the time of my visit in 1995, the justice committee was facilitating ongoing community participation in mediation and was acting in a sentence advisory capacity at the Provincial Court.

Perspectives of Community Members and Justice System Personnel on Developments at Pukatawagan

The Pukatawagan residents I interviewed were all members of the justice committee. Gabriel Bighetty commented on the impact of his committee on offender behaviour:

> Finally, a guy realizes that's [what] I should do and there's [a] lot of guys starting to change. Even the jailbirds, when they're coming in and they start fooling around like that, we talk to them, too. They're starting to slow down . . . and slow down, don't do that. We talk nicely.[35]

Bighetty also felt that too many Cree people were being sent to jail by the courts. He believed the justice committee was improving this situation by effecting changed behaviours among the offenders they dealt with.

Liz Bear viewed the justice committee as having empowered the community of Pukatawagan through promoting local participation in the justice system. She stressed her committee's focus on healing, treatment, and reconciliation, in contrast to the prevailing system's focus on punishment and incarceration. She stated:

> The focus over there for them is incarceration. That's the courts. They go by punishment for anything committed. We're saying, yes, there is some sort of punishment, but we're not going to send you out to jail. We're going to try and help you deal with it here. We listen to you. You offer some solutions

on how we can help you or what [you] would . . . rather see. You know you
have a choice here. You learn to quit your behaviour by going out and learn-
ing why you abuse. . . . [W]hat environment do you have to change in your
home? What do you have to work on? Are you committed to going to work
with somebody here?[36]

She also believed that local offenders would be more likely to accept treatment under the direction of the justice committee than through the Provincial Court:

Maybe if the justice committee made that recommendation it wouldn't sound
like such an order. When you get a court order to go to a rehab centre, there
is very much resistance . . . because they are being ordered to go. They only
go and satisfy that condition. They are not going there for themselves.[37]

Judge Martin had witnessed the evolution of community participation
in sentencing at Pukatawagan:

I was very impressed with not only what was said, but the fact that people
whom I had never heard speak before were able to air their feelings about
themselves, the community, what it needed, and whether or not it was relevant
to the sentencing process. It was worthwhile listening to these people. Often
they wouldn't deal directly with the accused himself or with the problem
associated with sentencing, but they would let me know in a general way just
how the community felt about that particular person and whether or not there
was any hope for rehabilitation and so forth. In a general way, as well, I found
the Aboriginal people in that community, notwithstanding its reputation for
violence, to be very forgiving and understanding of the problems of their
fellows.[38]

Although Judge Martin's involvement with local justice participation was
primarily in the context of hearing community representations on sentence
in court, he recognized the possibility of informal dispute-resolution tribunals in Aboriginal communities:

It is difficult to say where it might go from here, but I think without a con-
certed effort by our courts and/or the Aboriginal people themselves to form
their own courts or mediation boards or whatever might be the answer [it will
go nowhere]. But I do believe that some form of justice could easily be worked
on the reserve using elders as peacemakers so to speak, especially in family
disputes and things like that. They have the resources to order a person to take
anger management. They have the resources to give alcohol counselling and
so forth.[39]

Judge Martin said such tribunals would deal with minor offences, while more serious transgressions would be referred to a Crown attorney.

RCMP corporal Robert Brossart recognized a difference in focus between the prevailing justice system and the justice committee:

> I suppose each has got its pluses and minuses. . . . The justice committee itself trie[s] to work with the person to make them a better person. I've seen repeat offenders that have gone to the justice committee. I've seen them abuse and assault and re-assault. But then again, I've also seen that from the provincial courts. One system as opposed to the other, I don't know if one's better than the other. . . . The majority of the decisions from the justice committee, or all I've ever seen, are to get counselling, and there's no form of deterrent. As opposed to the provincial system, [where if] you do something wrong you get some community hours like we've seen this morning or a fine or [are] sentenced to jail. With the justice committee all it is is healing. They try to work with the person, make them a better person, and try to deal with it that way. [40]

While Corporal Brossart recognized the committee's focus on healing the offender, he questioned the degree of offender follow-up done by committee members. He stated: "The follow-up is really relaxed too. You can give any sentence you want, but if there's nobody to check or follow-up on that sentence, [it] makes it very difficult."[41]

Defence counsel Joyce Dalmyn noted varied opinions among offenders about the justice committee: some perceived the committee as the route to a lighter sentence or no sentence at all, yet others appeared to have genuinely benefitted from such community support and involvement. Her comments helped to contrast the mediation role played by the committee outside court with the sentence advisory role in court. She noted strategic considerations, as defence counsel, in deciding whether to seek in-court involvement of the justice committee as she would not want her client to be sentenced following this input unless she felt there were people on the committee and in the community who would be willing to speak out in favour of her client rather than remaining silent.[42]

Karen Dumas was the resident probation officer in April of 1995, and she sat in an advisory role on the justice committee. She noted that some probation orders directed offenders to report directly to the justice committee, and that the justice committee was consulted about and allowed input into the preparation of pre-sentence reports for the Provincial Court. She also commented that victim and offender involvement before the justice committee had helped to promote the healing process at Pukatawagan.[43]

3 | Evaluation and Thoughts for the Future

9 | The Development and Impact of Community Sentencing and Mediation Initiatives

Data from the Aboriginal communities studied yielded four approaches to community participation in the justice system: the sentencing circle, the elders' or community sentencing panel, the sentence advisory committee, and the community mediation committee. Case selection in all models was controlled by judges, with the exception of criminal mediation at Cumberland House and Pukatawagan.

A wide variety of offences were disposed of through the community sentencing and mediation approaches considered in this study. In northern Saskatchewan, the criterion requiring that a case be one on "which the court would be willing to take a calculated risk and depart from the usual range of sentencing" appeared to have had the effect of restricting circle sentencing to offences and offenders for which a period of incarceration considerably less than two years would have been the norm. Other than *Taylor*,[1] no Saskatchewan circle sentencing case involved a sexual assault, an offence that usually results in a penitentiary term according to appellate sentencing guidelines.

The sentencing circles conducted at Hollow Water were, by contrast, sexual assault cases. Although the local dynamics at Hollow Water were complex, the protocol negotiated with the Department of Justice appeared to have been a major factor in allowing community sentencing for an offence that previously had automatically resulted in an penitentiary term. The question whether certain offences, especially those involving domestic violence, were suitable for circle sentencing remained unanswered. Feminist scholarship has argued that the historical power imbalances existing in abusive relationships make violent men poor candidates for mediation,[2] yet cases of spousal assault were considered within sentencing circles in northern Saskatchewan. The consideration of such cases by circle sentencing, or by other community sentencing or mediation approaches, will require great caution to ensure the victim has significant support and that she has not been coerced into participating.

The sentencing and mediation approaches studied included Aboriginal traditions and practices to varying degrees. A prayer was offered in Cree by an elder both at the Pukatawagan court on April 11, 1995, and at the Pelican

Narrows circle. An Ojibway prayer was offered at the Waywayseecappo court on March 2, 1995, and at the Winnipeg circle. No prayer or traditional ceremony preceded the Cumberland House sentencing circle committee meeting on December 13, 1994. Sweet grass and pipe ceremonies were used during court at Hollow Water and Pukatawagan, and were also used during the Winnipeg circle. Offenders and other circle participants were allowed to speak their Native languages in all the court and mediation hearings I observed.

The Aboriginal practices incorporated into community sentencing and mediation included both spirituality (signified by prayers, the burning of sweet grass, and pipe ceremonies) and process (such as grassroots consultation, community consensus, and sharing). The circle itself has been viewed by Aboriginal people as having traditional significance. This point was made strongly by two sentencing circle participants: Berma Bushie, an Ojibway from Hollow Water,[3] and Verna Merasty, a Cree from Sandy Bay.[4] Whether or not such a specific historical link exists for the First Nations in this study, the circle format employed in court and mediation represented a more egalitarian process of adjudication, one that reflected the communal traditions and aspirations of Aboriginal society.

Although the Aboriginal practices described above formed an integral part of the sentencing process, their inclusion appeared to be more of an adaptation to conventional court protocol than an adoption of traditional Aboriginal dispute-resolution practices. Conventional Canadian adjudication practices were retained, with the judge controlling the final sentencing decision, and with the voices of defence and Crown counsel often predominant in an otherwise consultative process. Despite the continued prominence of judges and lawyers, these community sentencing approaches nevertheless demonstrated the flexibility of Canadian criminal law, in allowing local participation and in recognizing traditional Aboriginal practices during sentencing.

As all the initiatives studied were in their infancy, conclusions regarding their impact on offenders, victims, and communities were, at best, tentative and largely anecdotal. For example, lawyer Joyce Dalmyn described the positive impact of a sentencing circle on a young man at Pukatawagan:

> There are some [offenders], for example, the young man I mentioned earlier who should have been in a penitentiary and [would have] gotten no benefit there [and] who, for some reason, has done extremely well for two years. And I can't explain that. Did the input of the community help him? It must have. He spent three and a half out of the four preceding years in jail. Something good came [from the sentencing circle] for him. Is he an anomaly or is he a norm?[5]

During a sentencing circle conducted on April 19, 1995, at Sandy Bay, Judge Fafard stated that, although two offenders sentenced before local sentencing circles had re-offended, the result of such circles had generally been positive. He believed offenders paid more attention to recommendations from the community than from a judge alone. "Before sentencing circles, I would leave your community at the end of the day without solving any of the underlying problems," he told the circle.[6]

No data were available on recidivism rates for offenders dealt with through community sentencing or mediation in the communities studied. At Pukatawagan, Corporal Robert Brossart believed there had been little difference in recidivism between offenders sentenced in conventional court and those dealt with by the justice committee.[7] Although prominent cases of recidivism may have had the effect of fuelling opposition to community sentencing,[8] the usefulness of this measure in assessing the effectiveness of these reforms remains open to question, given the track record of the prevailing justice system in Aboriginal communities. As Judge Stuart of the Yukon Territorial Court noted, "Whatever failures the [Sentencing] Circle may experience, it is important to note how the justice system ha[s] failed numerous times with the same offender."[9]

To gauge the impact of these initiatives upon offenders, I interviewed participants in the initiatives and observed offenders in court or during mediation. I interviewed two former offenders in Sandy Bay, but I did not interview any offenders at the time of sentencing because most were preoccupied with their cases. On a field trip to Sandy Bay in October of 1994, I spoke with one of the first offenders sentenced before a local sentencing circle. I planned to interview him on a future visit, but when I returned to Sandy Bay in April of 1995, he was in jail for breaching a no-alcohol provision in his probation order. While I was there, I tried to interview the offender sentenced in the Sandy Bay circle, but he declined to be interviewed.

I did manage to interview several people who had participated in community sentencing circles. The participants I talked to believed they were better equipped to control offender behaviour than judges, lawyers, or probation officers. They viewed peer pressure during community sentencing and mediation as a significant factor in promoting changed offender behaviour.

The immediate effect of peer pressure upon offenders was evident at the Sandy Bay and Pelican Narrows circles and during court at Waywayseecappo and Pukatawagan. The offenders sentenced on these occasions appeared humbled by the experience of coming before other community members. Circle sentencing committee member Donald McKay, Jr., of Cumberland House described the impact of his committee:

If the community people begin to deal with the community problems, you know, and people being accused of these crimes will come in, they are pretty nervous to face the community, but this person has to live in this community. Whether they get probation or jail, they're going to come back and live here. So I just think if they deal with the community and realize people around the sentencing circle are trying to help them out, I think more and more people will ask for the sentencing circle.[10]

By involving community members in sentence design and supervision, judges made accessible additional resources to encourage behavioural reform and, at the same time, facilitated reconciliation among offenders, victims, and the local community. In *Joseyounen,* Judge Fafard commented:

The aim of sentencing circles is the same [as] when the disposition is arrived at by other means: the protection of society by curtailing the commission of the crime by this offender and others. However, in sentencing circles the emphasis is less on deterrence and more on re-integration into society, rehabilitation, and a restoration of harmony within the community.[11]

During a field trip to Sandy Bay in April 1995, I interviewed one former young offender, who had appeared before the Sandy Bay Youth Sentencing Advisory Committee. He described the positive impact this experience had had on him. When the committee had challenged him to explain the reason for his crime (a break and enter), he felt able to tell the committee about his troubled home life. He said the committee had helped him by exploring the problems underlying his behaviour and by providing him with ongoing support and counselling. At the time I spoke with him, he had not re-offended.

It was difficult for me to assess the impact of community sentencing and mediation initiatives upon crime victims. Out of respect for their situation, I did not interview any victims directly. I did get some information about their reactions from comments made by circle participants and by observing victims during circle sentencing and at the Hollow Water community review. CHCH at Hollow Water was the only initiative I studied that showed evidence of a formal support system for victims. Although the other community sentencing and mediation initiatives claimed to promote reconciliation between offenders and victims, the involvement of victims and provisions for victim support in these communities appeared disorganized and inconsistent.

Although victims were usually present at the formal and informal sentencing circles conducted at Pukatawagan, lawyer Joyce Dalmyn and

Corporal Robert Brossart questioned the lack of victim involvement in mediation conducted by the local justice committee.[12] In northern Saskatchewan, victim involvement in circle sentencing and mediation was inconsistent. Although the victim had been active in arranging and participated at the Sandy Bay circle, the victim was not present at the Pelican Narrows circle nor did anyone speak on his behalf.[13] At the sentencing circle committee meeting on December 13, 1994, at Cumberland House, no victims appeared before the committee, although some appeared to have been consulted previously by committee members. With the exception of CHCH at Hollow Water, victims appeared to have participated less and have had less support offered to them than offenders.

A major impact of these initiatives on the communities studied was the empowerment of the participants. Some viewed the development of community sentencing and mediation as essential to the health of their communities. At Cumberland House, sentencing circle committee chairperson Cyril Roy stated that expansion of his committee's role in local dispute resolution was the "only way we can keep our community a little stronger and keep it going."[14] Lawyer Felicia Daunt observed that the impact of circle sentencing at Sandy Bay had been empowering:

> Well, in Sandy Bay, in particular, I've noticed that sentencing circles have really had a very positive impact on the community. In Sandy Bay we used to see a lot more violent offences and higher levels of violence than you do now. In general, I get the impression that the community has started to heal itself, and I think sentencing circles were a step in that. It sort of got the people in the community together talking about problems that, although they're sentencing one person, the community shares.[15]

Despite these positive views, others I spoke with at Sandy Bay were sceptical of the impact of circle sentencing. Indeed, by the spring of 1995, a perception appeared to be developing among Sandy Bay offenders that sentencing circles were an easy way out. Sentencing circle participant Harry Morin viewed this development as resulting largely from the lack of treatment options available for offenders in northern Saskatchewan. This shortage often meant that a suspended sentence with few probation conditions was the only alternative to jail available for some offenders, leaving the impression that little if any penalty had been imposed. Criticism of the circle process was also heard at the Winnipeg circle when an Ojibway man, the brother of both victims, openly challenged the circle approach and suggested that the victims and the offender (his father) would have been better off if they had participated in a session with a trained psychologist as opposed to interacting with community members within the circle. Given such varied reactions and the short history of these initiatives, their longer term implications and impact remain difficult to assess. In the short term, however, such approaches have clearly had an empowering effect upon the community members involved in their development.

In my analysis of the community sentencing and mediation initiatives studied and the new approaches undertaken, I have utilized three theoretical frameworks: post-colonialism, legal pluralism, and popular justice. These frameworks provide further means towards understanding the reasons underlying dissatisfaction with the conventional system and understanding the implications of the changes to this system that have occurred in some Aboriginal communities.

10 | Post-Colonialism, Legal Pluralism, and Popular Justice

My research showed that Aboriginal people felt estranged from and disenchanted with the prevailing justice system. These feelings were reflected in, and were relevant to, problems associated with conventional sentencing practices. My research also showed that local systems of social control existed outside the formal court system and had an impact on the sentencing of offenders within it.

Post-Colonialism

The six Aboriginal communities I studied shared a history of European colonization. Scholars of post-colonialism examine the experiences of countries or communities following colonization. This branch of study is a useful tool to explain resistance to the justice system and conventional sentencing practices within these communities and to understand how Aboriginal people view justice and sentencing issues.

Criminal law has been described as pivotal to the colonization and domination of Indigenous Peoples. Peter Fitzpatrick, professor of Law and Social Theory at the University of Kent, stated:

> Operatively, the essence of colonization was concentrated in the criminal law. As a universalistic project imperial colonization made all that stood outside it provisional and strange. "Native society" in its whole range was rendered deviant, and the colonized rendered "presumptive criminals" [citations omitted]. Anything that resisted re-creation in imperialism's own terms was denied or suppressed.[1]

Colonialism has been defined in two ways within socio-legal literature: narrowly as a consideration of "European political, economic, and cultural expansion into Latin America, Africa, Asia and the Pacific during the last four hundred years," and more broadly as "a relation between two or more groups of unequal power in which one not only controls and rules the other but also endeavours to impose its cultural order onto the subordinate group(s)."[2] The broader definition is descriptive of the experience of

Canadian Aboriginal people, who were recipients of a criminal justice system imposed through colonization.

Although early studies of law and colonization stressed "the role of law in imperial domination," subsequent scholarship focussed on the means by which Indigenous populations "resisted and accommodated" colonization.[3] As an example of the latter focus, author Robert Kidder questioned earlier scholarship that suggested colonial law had simply been imposed by colonizers on less-powerful Indigenous populations. He argued that the degree to which colonial law had been successfully imposed upon such people depended largely on the degree of their resistance. He stated:

> The sheer inventiveness of supposedly imposed-upon populations not only warms the heart of those who cheer for underdogs; it suggests that the fact of imposition is itself questionable. At what point in the process of legal challenge and indigenous response do we conclude that law has been "imposed"?[4]

In a North American context, Professor Mike Brogden of Liverpool Polytechnic described various forms of resistance by the French Metis of western Canada to colonial authority during the nineteenth century and the resulting labels of criminality applied to the Metis in an effort to disable such opposition.[5]

Post-colonial writing has been based largely in the experience and practice of the European colonization of India, Africa, and Latin America. Much of the writing on law and colonization has been authored by anthropologists, historians, and social scientists who are themselves members of colonizing societies.[6] In response to a perceived Eurocentric bias on the part of such writers, a body of post-colonial literature authored by Indigenous writers, who analyse colonial history and dynamics from the perspective of the colonized, has emerged.[7] Such writing, usually characterized by acerbic and pointed critiques of European colonization, provides a link to the experiences and perspectives of many Aboriginal Canadians who express disenchantment with and estrangement from the Canadian justice system.

Professor Sally Merry of Wellesley College in Boston, Massachusetts, described a form of resistance currently in existence in some post-colonial countries that is highly relevant to the analysis of Canadian community sentencing initiatives:

> Some post-colonial countries are now experimenting with new forms of local justice that are now more rooted in customary law, more conciliatory, and more locally controlled as the more established local courts become more formalized and bureaucratic over time and replicate the forms of the colonial

courts. . . . Efforts to expand supervision, to develop formal procedures, and to reduce customary law to writing contradict efforts to reproduce local power relations and replicate a more informal, situationally informed vision of justice. *Courts designed in a capital city are very different when they are implemented in remote villages and towns, places not easily supervised by the centre and already dominated by a local elite. Local courts are, to use Sally Falk Moore's term . . . , semi-autonomous social fields: semi-independent social systems that develop local practices within a larger structure which constrains the way they function.*[8] [Emphasis added]

Resistance to the prevailing court system was in evidence within the communities I studied, both in perspectives expressed and local actions taken. All the communities had experienced estrangement from the prevailing court system: the system was viewed by many as external to and separate from their communities. Many people I interviewed believed local community members were better equipped than the court system to control offender behaviour and should, therefore, be given a greater role in the sentencing and supervision of offenders.

In seeking to understand community sentencing and mediation, it is essential to consider these "local" points of view. Professor Sherry Ortner of the University of California, Berkeley, has argued that many ethnographic studies of colonial dominance and resistance have suffered from a lack of Indigenous perspectives. She claims Indigenous perspectives facilitate an understanding of community political dynamics, inherent cultural richness, and local perceptions about the interaction between colonial and Indigenous people.[9] I have attempted in this book to include as many personal perspectives of Aboriginal people as possible. These viewpoints come from a variety of local community members whose voices have rarely been heard in analyses of the criminal justice system. I hope these perspectives will provide some insight into how the criminal justice system may be adapted and made more effective in Aboriginal communities.

In the course of this study, I found active resistance to the prevailing court system at Pukatawagan, where, for a period of eight months in 1993, all spousal assault cases were diverted from court to the local justice committee because witnesses refused to testify at trial. Earlier resistance had been seen at Pukatawagan when, during the mid-1980s and fuelled by local dissatisfaction with the Provincial Court, this First Nation passed a bylaw forbidding the court party from entering their reserve. In 1997, the Mathias Colomb Band once again forbade the court party from entering the reserve. In Pelican Narrows, sentencing circle committee member Cecile Merasty described resistance by offenders who remained passive and refused to participate in conventional sentencing before the court.[10] Such resistance was evidence of a lack of understanding and a mistrust or rejection of the prevailing system.

Given this history of estrangement from and resistance to institutions introduced and imposed by colonization, it is not surprising that people living in remote Aboriginal communities have a different relationship to the justice system from those living in larger, non-Aboriginal centres. Police influence in isolated Aboriginal communities appeared to be limited largely to peace-keeping. Corporal Bob MacMillan of Pelican Narrows explained:

> Even though they don't really care for us, they know we're impartial. And they trust us in that regard. They don't really like us, but they know we're not going to choose sides based on family. . . . But that's where [the line is] drawn, it's finished. . . . [O]utside of arresting people . . . we have very little influence in this town. We go to the school and give them a lecture on drugs. Pooh! You might as well play a video, because they have no interest in what we say. None. It's not like in a southern community, where the RCMP are involved with the community as such, because here we're not part of the community, we're outsiders. White people as a rule are outsiders in Pelican Narrows.[11]

This passage clearly reflects the imposed nature of Canadian criminal law in these communities. Judge Fafard repeatedly commented on his court's lack of credibility among local residents. This was reflected in the comments of several community members who expressed dissatisfaction with judges and probation officers who attended in their communities only one or two days a month and left immediately after court.

Many within these communities felt the prevailing justice system was focussed on punishment through imprisonment. By contrast, local perspectives favoured reconciling offenders with victims and the community, and healing the underlying causes of deviant behaviour. Jail was viewed largely as a place where offenders became bitter. After a period of incarceration, they would return to their home communities untreated with their underlying problems unresolved.

It was evident during the course of this study that the Aboriginal focus was on overall community welfare. Pukatawagan justice committee member Liz Bear reflected on this:

> This is our community and it is dysfunctional. You can't deny that. It is dysfunctional because of the alcohol abuse, the lack of our social and economic means, and everything like that, but it is home. Let's heal here. Let's build a healthier community. And if we can do that, those behaviours are going to stop one way or another.[12]

This communal focus sometimes appeared at odds with the focus on individual rights within the conventional Canadian justice system. At Hollow Water, Berma Bushie said that upon receiving a sexual assault disclosure, the CHCH assessment team was able to determine quickly whether the complaint was true because of the team's experience with the people involved. If they believed the complainant, the accused would immediately be confronted by the assessment team and be given a chance to admit the abuse. Although dealing with the question of guilt and not sentencing, this example discloses a very different concept of the rights of the accused and the presumption of innocence than exists within the conventional system.

It may seem odd that community members actively participated in community sentencing initiatives that operated within a system they appeared to reject. This may reflect the achievement (either apparent or real) by community sentencing of some of the goals that, it is claimed, ordinary sentencing and incarceration processes do not achieve: reconciliation, healing, and community empowerment. The community sentencing and mediation initiatives in this study represent adaptations to conventional sentencing practices. These adaptations reflect the sensitivity of judges to local concerns about the inadequacies of prevailing sentencing practices and, most significantly, the power of local communities to facilitate change through resistance to the prevailing system. This judicial creativity is reminiscent of the creation of "customary law" by European colonial authority in Asia and Africa. As an example of this latter form of imposition, Francis Snyder, professor of European Community law at the European University Institute in Florence, argued that, in the context of the French colonization of Senegal, the law respecting land usage, which has been referred to as "customary law" in the twentieth century, was not based on local tradition but rather was created at the time of the colonial imposition of the capitalist state.[13] In the end, whether community sentencing and mediation were judicially introduced is not as significant as whether these reforms were accepted and supported by local residents.

While the effects of colonization are wide ranging and, to a great extent, explain Aboriginal resistance to the conventional justice system, a further level of enquiry is required to more completely understand the dynamics at work within the initiatives and approaches studied in this book. This requires a focus on the systems of informal law and social control that exist at the local community level, yet are outside the formal justice system.

Legal Pluralism

Another theoretical framework that facilitates the analysis of community sentencing and mediation is "legal pluralism." The dynamics of colonization are closely tied to the inter-relationship between local and state systems of law and social control. Legal pluralism focusses less on the historical aspects of colonization than on this inter-relationship. It is thus a useful tool in analysing specific sentencing initiatives and their relationship to local and state systems.

Professor Sally Merry defined legal pluralism as "a situation in which two or more legal systems coexist in the same social field [citations omitted]."[14] Sociologist Stuart Henry stated, "Legal pluralism . . . holds that every society contains a plurality of legal orders and legal subsystems (or fragments of these)."[15] This statement of legal pluralism recognizes the interaction between formal, state-imposed and local, indigenous systems of law and social control. As the sentencing initiatives under consideration in this study facilitated involvement of local community members in a process previously dominated by outside justice professionals, interaction between these systems was inevitable.

Social-control theorist Donald Black postulated an inverse relationship between the strength of local social control and dependence upon a formal legal code.[16] He traced modern reduction in social influence by the family within industrialized nations:

> In modern societies such as America, however, family control is weaker than in more traditional societies. With modernization it has weakened everywhere, and everywhere law has correspondingly increased. In Taiwan, for instance, the *tsu,* or clan, has steadily lost its former authority. Its sanctions have been undermined by changes in land tenure, and the growth of economic relationships outside the village has made its jurisdiction less relevant anyway. Other social control in the village has also declined. As all of this has happened, Taiwanese peasants have more and more turned to the police and courts [citation omitted]. The same pattern has appeared in every part of the world, gradually in some societies, quickly, even suddenly in others. In Europe, it happened over centuries. For many Indians of North America, it happened almost overnight, as quickly as they were moved to reservations [citations omitted]. In most of Africa, Asia, Latin America, and Oceania, it has come only recently, if at all. In Africa, for instance, family control is still so strong that juvenile law hardly exists.[17]

This tension between local and state systems of social control was also considered by Robert Ellickson, professor of law at Yale University, in his study of relations between cattle ranchers in Shasta County, California.[18] He found that, despite considerable statutory regulation of the cattle industry, problems such as cattle trespass and boundary-fence disputes were not dealt with by the processes of formal law but rather through local mechanisms of social control. These included such self-help measures as "negative gossip and mild physical reprisals."[19] He theorized that people often choose custom over formal law, in large part because "the substantive content of customary rules is more likely to be welfare maximizing" for members of the local community.

All the sentencing initiatives considered in this book were characterized by an increase in local community participation in the sentencing process. Rupert Ross commented on a similar move towards local community justice among the Cree and Ojibway of northwestern Ontario:

> The cries for local control over community justice are growing. It is tempting to conclude that they spring only from political claims of sovereignty, incidental only to the larger issue of political autonomy. While that may indeed form part of the background, it appears that much more is at stake in their eyes; the contribution which local control over justice would make, directly and indirectly, to the very goal of peaceful co-existence to which our system aspires.[20]

The literature on legal pluralism is a valuable starting point for analysing the relationship of the state and local systems of social control that exist in Aboriginal communities. Judge Sinclair highlighted an important aspect of this relationship in the distinction he made between community-, offender-, and judge-driven approaches to sentencing.[21] As an example of an offender-driven process, Judge Sinclair referred to a circle held in his court in December of 1993 at Winnipeg. He believed the process in that case was ineffective as the offender requested the circle and was responsible for bringing most of the people to the circle. As a result, the process was offender- and not community-driven.[22]

Justice initiatives may also be analysed by the prevailing philosophy employed within each. Rupert Ross distinguished community justice initiatives on the basis of proximity and adherence to competing paradigms, which he defined as "aboriginal healing" as opposed to "western criminal justice."[23] In contrasting the sentencing initiatives at Sandy Lake and at Attawapiskat, Ontario, with that at Hollow Water, Manitoba, he characterized the Hollow Water approach as more closely aligned with the Aboriginal healing paradigm, and he viewed the other initiatives as more closely tied to the state-controlled Western justice paradigm. The origins of sentencing initiatives may predict whether sentencing reforms evolve towards a distinctive local justice system or are simply assimilated into the established Canadian court system. An example of the positioning of a community-based justice initiative between the formal state legal system and traditional Indigenous law can be found in a proposal made by the Gitksan and Wet'suwet'en to the British Columbia government:

The justice system brought to Canada by the Europeans has been very disruptive of both the individual and community life of its Aboriginal people. We propose to implement an alternative in Northwestern B.C. that will allow the dispute resolution laws and methods of the Gitksan and Wet'suwet'en people to interact with the provincial justice system in a way that does not undermine the integrity of either.[24]

The discussion in this chapter has analyzed Aboriginal sentencing and mediation initiatives in terms of the effect of European colonization upon Aboriginal communities and in terms of local systems of social control and informal law. A final level of enquiry is whether the evolution of these initiatives and approaches parallels, to some extent, the development of other unconventional justice processes across North America and around the world.

Popular Justice

Yet another way of interpreting the development of community-based justice initiatives in Canadian Aboriginal communities is through the writing of Professor Sally Merry. In her study of community justice in California, she described "a move to popular justice." Her study of the San Francisco Community Boards program, a community-based justice approach begun in 1977, observed that popular justice initiatives are characterized by processes that are "informal in ritual and decorum, nonprofessional in language and personnel, local in scope, and limited in jurisdiction."[25] She described the role of popular justice initiatives in countries with an Anglo-American legal system. Given the similarities in evolution and development between the American and Canadian criminal justice systems, her analysis is equally applicable to the conventional Canadian system:

In countries with Anglo-American legal systems, popular justice is described as the opposite to an adversarial, rights-based, act-oriented legal system. . . . Many Third World countries equipped with colonial Anglo-American legal systems are developing customary-law forms of popular justice to reclaim a law suppressed during the colonial era. Procedures are conciliatory rather than adversarial, the characteristics of the Anglo-American legal system.[26]

A key element in the analysis of popular or community justice initiatives is their relationship to formal state law and local or indigenous systems of social control. Professor Merry theorized that "popular justice is best conceived as a legal institution located on the boundary between state law and indigenous or local law." She said that "[i]t can be thought of as intermediate, distinct from each side but linked to each."[27] Professor Peter

Fitzpatrick also analysed popular justice initiatives and argued that popular justice is best described as an adjunct of formal state control: popular justice programs complement formal state law by fulfilling roles not addressed by the latter.[28] Despite the difference in emphasis, both Fitzpatrick and Merry recognize an important link between popular justice and formal state control; they differ on the degree to which popular justice initiatives intersect with and represent indigenous or local law and social control.

Professor Merry distinguished several popular justice traditions that have developed in the twentieth century. Two of these, the "reformist" and "communitarian" traditions, are directly applicable to the current analysis of community sentencing initiatives. Reformist approaches are described as endeavouring to "increase the efficiency of the formal legal system by streamlining it and increasing its accessibility."[29] This approach seeks to increase "participation in modern legal institutions" and revise procedures.[30] Control over the reformist approach resides solely with the central state.[31] In contrast, communitarian approaches are described as being more closely related to "indigenous ordering than to state law."[32] This approach:

> seeks to operate entirely outside the state and its institutions. Communitarian popular justice is sometimes part of a withdrawal from secular society, an attempt to create a new religious or utopia[n] social order. Communitarian popular justice tribunals typically develop in small communities that are explicitly dedicated to maintaining a separate legal order and moral code.[33]

The community sentencing and mediation initiatives in this study demonstrate a conjunctive relationship between local Aboriginal communities and the Canadian justice system and therefore are more closely aligned with reformist than communitarian approaches. Several findings illustrate this inter-relationship. At Hollow Water, the threat of being charged under the *Criminal Code* with breach of probation (or undertaking) was an inducement for offenders to continue their treatment within CHCH. At Waywayseecappo, offenders were regularly ordered by the judge, or a justice of the peace, to attend a meeting of the elders' council as a term of their release. At Pelican Narrows, Pukatawagan, and Cumberland House, all local committees limited the number of opportunities for offenders to appear before them before "turning them back" to the conventional court system.

11 | Justice and Policy Issues Raised by Community Sentencing and Mediation

This study has identified several key issues, the resolution of which, both at the local community level and across the Canadian justice system as a whole, will affect the evolution of community sentencing and mediation in Aboriginal communities. These recurrent themes increase the inter-relationship, and at times the tension, between local systems of social control and the conventional justice system.

The following discussion focusses on the major policy issues raised in this study and the implications of each for reform of the criminal justice system in Canadian Aboriginal communities.

The Court's Supervisory Role in Community Sentencing Approaches

The development of sentence advisory committees at Sandy Bay, Pelican Narrows, and Cumberland House are evidence of a move away from circle sentencing with a judge in attendance towards developing community sentencing recommendations in the absence of the court party. This reduces the amount of court time required for such cases, but raises the issue of the court's role in such a progression: should it simply receive sentencing recommendations from a community committee or should it actively facilitate consensus in sentencing circles? Judge Stuart of the Yukon Territorial Court expressed concern about the absence of judges within the sentencing circle process. He viewed a judge's presence as the preferred means of identifying and controlling power imbalances between circle participants, although he recognized that such a role could also be performed by a community member.[1] While supporting the sentence advisory committee approach, Judge Fafard recognized the need for periodic judicial involvement in such circles, to ensure consistency and forestall potential misuse of the process:

> I guess I want to ensure some consistency, you know, because you have several accused charged with the same or similar offences. I want to make sure that the dispositions are fairly consistent. But I guess the greater thing is that it affects so many different people in that one community, that I'm almost afraid of some political influence. Because it touches on so many people, and I just

sort of felt that maybe I should be there to ensure that politics doesn't get involved, that you don't have a powerful family dictating to a weaker family, that kind of thing.[2]

Despite this judicial caution over power imbalances, trained and experienced community members might eventually perform the facilitation function currently performed by judges during circle sentencing. Indeed, at the sentencing circle committee meeting I attended on December 13, 1994, at Cumberland House, committee chairperson Cyril Roy performed a facilitation role similar to that performed by Judge Fafard at the Pelican Narrows and Sandy Bay circles. Judge Stuart described the use of community members as circle sentencing facilitators in the Yukon in the following terms:

> In some communities, the presiding Judge or Justice of the Peace act as facilitators. Other communities have persons as "Keepers of the Circle" who act both as host and facilitator of the Circle process. If a "Keeper of the Circle" is not a Justice of the Peace, the "Keeper" will call upon the Judge or Justice of the Peace to handle all legal matters required throughout the Hearing.[3]

At a community review circle conducted on February 22, 1995, at Hollow Water (during which the progress of five offenders and victims previously dealt with through sentencing circles was evaluated), community member Marcel Hardesty acted as a facilitator for the victim, offenders, and community members in attendance.

Although judges provide protection from power imbalances during court, the court party regularly departs these communities after court, leaving community circle participants to deal directly with offenders in the court's absence, either immediately or upon the offender's return from jail. As a result, development of mediation and facilitation skills could strengthen the local, informal systems of social control that attempt to change offender behaviour and promote rehabilitation.

An ongoing consideration in analysing community sentencing and mediation approaches is whether a distinction should be drawn between legitimate community support and advocacy for an offender, on the one hand, and political interference with the judicial process by a local participant, on the other. The following section deals with the difficult question of how "judicial independence," thought by many to be the cornerstone of our criminal justice system, is to be ensured while, at the same time, increasing the participation of offenders, victims, and community members.

Political Influence and Judicial Independence

Community sentencing and mediation involve interaction between local systems of social control and the formal justice system. In evolving community sentencing and mediation initiatives, the Canadian criminal court system, based on the principle of judicial independence from political interference and coercion, interacts with the opinions, informal relationships, and power structures of local communities. Local politics and the popularity and status of specific offenders can have an impact on community sentencing. Judge Fafard, in expressing concern for the integrity and independence of circle sentencing, was adamant that power imbalances resulting from political influence be avoided, thereby preventing actual or perceived bias. In *Joseyounen* he wrote:

> In the Euro-Canadian model where the judge imposes sentence without the aid of a sentencing circle, the judge speaks for the people and attempts to deliver a fair, impartial and just disposition. This he does without fear of political interference while at the same time he attempts to reflect the legitimate concerns and aspirations of the community. . . . In exploring the flexibility of the criminal law of Canada and its ability to accommodate First Nations cultures and legitimate needs, let us not re-invent those things which are so important to an impartial system of justice. If we throw out the essence of impartiality we run the risk of doing grave injustice to both offender and victim. What I mean is the input of community elders and leaders must not mean the exercise of political influence in the circle to the detriment of the accused or a victim. . . . The principle of judicial independence in decision-making is one that is deeply ingrained in the Canadian population, including the First Nations. The many sentencing circles I have held have included the participation of chiefs, band councillors, mayors, and others in political office. I have never seen any of these persons attempt to influence the outcome by virtue of their political office.[4]

I observed no direct attempts at political influence through representations at community sentencing circles, although the potential for such interference necessitates caution. Associate Chief Judge Giesbrecht of the Provincial Court of Manitoba, while conducting an enquiry under the *Fatal Inquiries Act* of Manitoba, found numerous examples of political interference by chiefs and councillors in the operation of the Dakota Ojibway Child and Family Services.[5] Judge Giesbrecht described the following examples of political influence within two reserve communities:

> - Constable Ralph Roulette of the Ontario Provincial Police Force described an incident that occurred at the Birdtail Sioux Reserve when he was a constable with DOTC [the Dakota Ojibway Tribal Council] Police. Mr. Roulette had evidence that the chief's son was guilty of the offence of impaired driving. The chief ordered Mr. Roulette not to charge his son. . . .

- Constable Edward Riglin of the Brandon City Police described incidents of political interference that took place when he was a constable with DOTC Police from 1986 to 1990. Constable Riglin was personally threatened with a band council resolution (BCR) banning him from the reserve on a number of occasions because he insisted on charging influential reserve residents with criminal offences.[6]

While these examples point to the dangers of local political interference, it should also be remembered that judges and other participants in the justice system are not free of personal biases.[7] Such biases are likely to play some role, either directly or indirectly, within the sentencing process.

Closely related to, and at times indistinguishable from, questions of local political interference, is the effect of offender popularity and status on the sentencing process. These appeared to be significant factors in the developing initiatives, especially at Pukatawagan. Lawyer Joyce Dalmyn explained that judges sitting at this First Nation were significantly influenced by a lack of community support for an offender:

> Sometimes people have nothing to say, which can be very unfortunate. And that's something as defence counsel I have to alert my client to, is if they want to have a circle, they had better make sure that they're going to have someone there to speak for them. Because if the feather gets passed around and no-one makes any comment whatsoever, I have heard a judge state, right on the record, "Well, it's clear that because nothing has been said, obviously they're not willing to say anything good about this person therefore I can only draw the conclusion that there's no sympathy for this person and I have to use the harshest penalties available to me."[8]

This raises the possibility of community bias against unpopular or marginalized offenders. This occurred in *R. v. Howard*,[9] where the British Columbia Court of Appeal reduced a sentence that had been unfairly aggravated by community animosity. The court commented that "the sentencing hearing had turned into an extended post hoc attack upon the accused when the sentencing judge permitted anyone who wished to comment on the accused's character or the impact of the [victim's] death on the native community to be heard."[10]

The conventional Canadian court system has evolved as a buffer between offenders and the harshness of public and victim reaction to their crimes. Indeed, one of the tenets of the formal court system is avoidance of personal reprisal by victims, or their agents, against perpetrators. Author T. Marshall wrote: "The historical antecedents of our criminal adjudication system suggest that its main purpose is to preserve public order by substituting state sanction for private vengeance.[citation omitted]"[11] A valid concern regarding these community sentencing and mediation approaches is that local involvement should not become a forum for the application of political pressure to the advantage of local elites and to the detriment of politically unpopular or marginalized offenders or victims. In the future, when judges seek community participation in sentencing without the consent of offenders or victims, judicial vigilance will be required to ensure community comments and recommendations are not motivated by political considerations. This may prove a difficult task for the judge, who, as an outsider to the community, may not be able to recognize the often subtle and non-verbal forms of intervention and influence that may be present.

A related challenge will be determining the line between political influence, on the one hand, and community support, on the other. In the Saskatchewan communities studied, there had to be an indication of local support for the offender before a sentencing circle was formed, making negative bias unlikely. Indeed, any bias was likely to be in favour of rather than against the offender. This leaves open the potential problem of inter-family politics. Before the Sandy Bay circle, the offender's family met outside the court, apparently concerned about the number of non-family community members and outsiders in attendance. At the start of the circle, family members questioned whether non-family should be allowed to participate, suggesting an attempt by this family to control the sentencing process. As the circle was open to the public, Judge Fafard refused to disqualify anyone from the circle.

Despite the variety of potential problems that are raised by direct community input at sentencing, personal relationships between circle participants and the offender—although representing a lack of objectivity and a partiality towards offender support and rehabilitation—do provide the court with a better understanding of the problems causing or contributing to the offender's behaviour. These relationships also increase the resources available to a court in attempting to control and change such behaviour.

For community sentencing and mediation initiatives to evolve, it is clear that the concern over local political interference must be addressed. A broader political consideration is the extent to which public funding should assist in this evolution. The following section considers competing viewpoints on the propriety of volunteer support versus government funding in the local justice system.

Financial Infrastructure or Volunteer Support?

To what degree should community sentencing and mediation initiatives be supported by government funding as opposed to the voluntary efforts of citizens? Lawyer Sid Robinson of La Ronge viewed a financial infrastructure as essential to the evolution of circle sentencing in northern Saskatchewan. Financial compensation for justice committee members who sat with the court was raised as a significant issue at Pukatawagan, as explained by justice committee member Theresa Bighetty:

> When the court time [came] the justice committee don't go in the court because we don't get paid. That's why they don't like to go there—don't want to sit there for nothing. . . . Well, everybody likes to get paid when they do something. . . . This thing is not really settled yet. I remember I got paid a couple times there going on the court dates. I get paid just a couple of times. But before that, we didn't get paid before that.[12]

Judge Fafard, however, viewed payment as interfering with the independence of the court and preferred circle sentencing in northern Saskatchewan to continue developing through the dedication of community volunteers.

Although community and volunteer support was essential to the continued success of all initiatives, financial resources to train and pay support staff and establish treatment facilities contributed significantly to the development of several of the community initiatives studied. At Pelican Narrows, participation by most members of the sentencing circle committee was facilitated through their employment with the Peter Ballantyne Band. The committee's chairperson, Derek Custer, managed this committee as part of his assigned employment duties. At Waywayseecappo, additional government funding supported the movement of court from Rossburn to the reserve, the employment of an Aboriginal person as a resident probation officer, and payment of a per diem allowance for the elders sitting in court. At Hollow Water, most members of the CHCH assessment team were social workers employed by various levels of government.

A shortage of treatment facilities in northern Saskatchewan, and a lack of money to build them, appears to have slowed the development of circle sentencing in that region since 1995. According to Sandy Bay resident and sentencing circle participant Harry Morin, a shortage of accessible treatment resources has limited the sentencing options for repeat offenders.[13] The expansion of support and treatment resources appears essential to the evolution of all community sentencing and mediation initiatives.

Debates over public funding for such initiatives are likely to continue. Closely related to the issue of public funding is the extent to which the unconventional sentencing and mediation practices considered in this study are to be used in dealing with the myriad of charges that are laid throughout the criminal justice system.

Expansion of Community Sentencing Approaches

Another issue identified through this study is the breadth of application and potential for the expansion of community sentencing and mediation approaches. For example, are local representatives to be involved in all sentencing at court, as in the elders' council at Waywayseecappo, or only in specific cases, as in all other communities studied? Realistically, even assuming the appropriateness of circle sentencing for all offenders, current court resources in the northern Saskatchewan and Manitoba communities studied were insufficient to allow circle sentencing for every offender facing sentencing, given the time requirements of circle sentencing.[14] A significant increase in court funding (which appears unlikely) or a move towards the sentence advisory committee model or the elders' sentencing panel model seem to be the options available for making community sentencing available to more offenders.

Despite the attention attracted by the development of circle sentencing in northern Saskatchewan, these circles represented a very small percentage of the sentencing occurring. During the Sandy Bay court sitting on April 19, 1995, one sentencing circle was conducted and approximately thirty other offenders were sentenced in the conventional fashion. A further option to facilitate community participation in the justice system is broader-based diversion to local mediation committees. This option, to some extent, will depend on the range of offences allowed to be diverted by provincial regulation. It will also depend on the willingness of Crown prosecutors to refer cases for mediation.

A related question about the breadth of community justice initiatives is whether community sentencing approaches could be used in larger, less isolated, and more ethnically diverse communities. All initiatives studied were located in small and relatively isolated Aboriginal communities. In *Morin,*[15] the court directed a sentencing circle for a Metis man from Saskatoon after representations of support were made by the local Metis community. Although no definition of "community" has been rendered judicially so as to restrict the application of circle sentencing or other community participation approaches, one strength of the sentencing initiatives studied was the ability of local community members to influence offender behaviour both during and after sentencing. Corporal Bob MacMillan of Pelican Narrows suggested local social control was more easily identified and accessed in smaller and more isolated communities than in the larger urban centres:

> You can't have a . . . sentencing circle in Saskatoon that would work. I can't see how it would work, because who are the community that's going to be dealing with the offender? You're going to go to Saskatoon and you're going to find a few elders somewhere that will come to a sentencing circle, impose whatever they feel is right for the accused, but then there's no follow-up. Who have these people got to go to? The rest of the community doesn't even know about it. Nor do they care.[16]

Although community-based sentencing and mediation has not been precluded in larger mixed centres, the social control that can be brought to bear on offenders in small communities is a strength.

Whether these community sentencing and mediation approaches will become established within non-Aboriginal communities is unclear. These approaches have evolved within Aboriginal communities largely in reaction to problems experienced with, and by, the prevailing justice system, and they have utilized the strength of local resources and systems of social control in the sentencing process. Although these approaches appear well suited to the communal traditions of Aboriginal society, nothing within Canadian law prevents non-Aboriginal offenders from seeking local sentencing input. There is no reason to believe the same degree of concern and social control could not be found and applied among identifiable communities in non-Aboriginal society. Indeed, two recent sentencing circle cases from Saskatchewan involved non-Aboriginal offenders: a non-Aboriginal offender charged with stealing a snowmobile attended a sentencing circle involving "the judge, lawyers, police and about a handful of Katepwa residents";[17] and a local farmer charged with dangerous driving causing death received a suspended sentenced following a sentencing circle.[18]

In addition to the nature and size of the community involved and to the level of volunteer and government support received, a further factor clearly will affect the evolution of community sentencing and mediation. The extent to which the criminal law, as defined in the *Criminal Code* and as interpreted through our appellate courts, allows or restricts application of these approaches will obviously affect their development.

The Potential Effect of Statutory Reform and Appellate Sentencing Review on the Development of Community Sentencing

The power of judges to involve community participants in the sentencing process has been based in the broad discretion given to judges within Canadian criminal law. No specific reference to community participation in sentencing, by sentencing circle or other means, appears in the *Criminal Code,* although section 723(3) provides that "[t]he court may . . . require production of evidence that would assist it in determining the appropriate sentence,"[19] and section 717 of the *Code* establishes a framework for "alternative measures," that is to say, diversion of offenders from the court system.[20] Regardless of these provisions, judges are clearly authorized to involve community members and victims in the sentencing process, making statutory reform unnecessary to the continued development of these approaches.

One statutory change that may affect the evolution of these approaches is the conditional sentence of imprisonment. As of September 3, 1996, the *Criminal Code* was amended to permit a court that imposed a sentence of imprisonment of less than two years, and which was satisfied that service of that sentence in the community would not endanger the community's safety, to direct that the sentence be served in the community subject to the conditions of a conditional sentence order. This amendment has allowed some offenders, who previously would have been facing an all-but-certain period of jail, to remain at home and access local resources identified through community sentencing processes.

The conditional sentence of imprisonment, however, does not apply to offences that require a minimum term of imprisonment, such as a subsequent conviction for impaired driving. In addition, effective May 2, 1997, Parliament amended this provision to require, in addition to being satisfied that community safety would not be endangered, that the court must also be satisfied that a conditional sentence would be "consistent with the fundamental purpose and principles of sentencing set out in sections 718 to 718.2." This may serve to restrict the number of conditional sentences granted, especially if significant weight is given to the sentencing principles of denunciation, deterrence, and parity, as these are often cited by Crown prosecutors and appellate courts in justifying jail sentences as opposed to community-based dispositions. An example of a restrictive view towards the use of conditional sentences can be found in *R.* v. *Brady,*[21] where Chief Justice Fraser of the Alberta Court of Appeal interpreted the number of community service hours that can accompany a conditional sentence (240) as indicating that Parliament intended this form of sentence for "relatively less serious offenders, or first-time offenders, or those who commit minor crimes."[22]

The Saskatchewan Court of Appeal, first in *Morin*[23] and then in *Taylor,*[24] is the only Canadian appellate court to have commented in any depth on the practice of circle sentencing.[25] A major difference of opinion was evident within that court. In *Morin*, the majority, led by Justice Sherstobitoff, although recognizing the legality and appropriateness of circle sentencing in some circumstances, clearly viewed the court's over-riding consideration to be sentence parity and, hence, whether any extraordinary circumstances distinguished this case from the normal appellate range, given the offender and the circumstances of the offence.[26] Chief Justice Bayda, in a strong dissent, argued that the principle of sentence parity must defer, in some cases, to attempts at ameliorating the over-representation of Aboriginal people in jail. He viewed circle sentencing as a tool to address this inequity and argued that "the perpetuation of entrenched attitudes in relation to sentencing in the guise of maintaining sentence parity is not in the interests of the administration of justice in this province or the well-being of our society."[27] In an interesting decision from the Yukon Territorial Court following *Morin,* Chief

Judge Lilles, in *C.P.*,[28] appeared to criticize what he viewed as the Saskatchewan Court of Appeal's preoccupation with sentence parity in determining the propriety of a sentencing circle for the offender. Judge Lilles commented that there are many advantages to community consultation through a sentencing circle, regardless of whether the sentence imposed is one of incarceration within the range "expected in ordinary court."

In *Taylor*, the Saskatchewan Court Appeal was again divided on the appropriateness of a sentencing circle. The offender had been convicted after trial on charges of sexual assault, uttering a death threat, and assault. He had spent a total of nine months in custody on remand before being sentenced. Despite his not-guilty plea and his denial of guilt while testifying at the trial, he sought and was granted a sentencing circle. The victim was initially not in favour of such a process but did eventually, if reluctantly, attend the circle. After two meetings of the sentencing circle, and based on a proposal by the local justice committee, the judge released the offender on an undertaking, including conditions that banished him to a remote island for one year and adjourned sentencing for this one year.

The Crown appealed the decision, which resulted in a direction from the Court of Appeal that sentencing not be delayed further. After six months on the island, the offender was again brought before the circle. Based on the recommendations of the circle, reached by a consensus of all members except the Crown prosecutor, the judge sentenced the offender to ninety days in jail to be followed by three years' probation. The probationary term included a condition banishing him for a further six months.

Chief Justice Bayda, with Justice Jackson concurring, although expressing some concerns about the formation of the circle without the initial consent of the victim and about whether the offender was truly remorseful, held that the process was valid as it "was saved by the attitude, conduct, and thinking of the circle participants who were the principal authors and creators of the sentence which the trial judge approved and adopted as his own."[29] Citing the Supreme Court of Canada's decision in *McDonnell*, Chief Justice Bayda found the "fact that the offence is serious sexual assault does not automatically rule out a sentencing circle."[30] He also found the sentence imposed by the trial judge after the circle to be fit.

Justice Cameron, however, argued that this was not an appropriate case for a sentencing circle, especially given the nature of the offence and the victim's reluctance to participate. He found the judge erred in acting on the circle's recommendation and that the sentence imposed was unfit, considering the gravity of the offender's conduct and the principle of parity (which required a starting-point sentence of three years' imprisonment for a sexual assault of this severity). Whether subsequent appellate comment adheres strictly to maintenance of established sentencing ranges and tariffs, on the one hand, or deference to the sentencing decisions taken by trial judges, on the other, will undoubtedly affect the development and scope of circle sentencing and other forms of community participation at sentencing.

As one aim of the community sentencing approaches considered in this study was to change offender behaviour through community reintegration rather than a jail term, many sentences achieved through these initiatives have fallen outside accepted appellate ranges. This has drawn criticism from those espousing the goal of provincewide sentence uniformity.[31] However, such arguments have failed to take account of the availability and effect of local resources, including informal systems of social control and offender support, within Aboriginal communities. These resources have provided a wider range of sentencing options.

The philosophy behind these developing initiatives has run counter to the prevailing assumption that more severe penalties (including prolonged incarceration) provide greater general and specific deterrence than community-based sentences. The community of Hollow Water disagreed with this assumption:

> The legal system, based on principles of punishment and deterrence, as we see it, simply is not working. We can not understand how the legal system doesn't see this. Whatever change that occurs when people return to the community from jail seems to be for the worse. Incarceration may be effective in the larger society, but it is not working in our community.[32]

In the communities studied, Crown support of community sentencing in general and of specific sentences awarded was essential, as a Crown appeal could result in the imposition of a harsher sentence in accordance with any relevant appellate sentencing tariff. Of the many sentencing circles that Judge Fafard had conducted in northern Saskatchewan by the time of this study, few had been appealed by the Crown. This was largely due to his insurance of Crown support before directing specific cases to a sentencing circle.

A further, and apparently as-yet-unaddressed question is whether the *Charter of Rights and Freedoms*[33] applies to these community sentencing approaches. Does an offender have a constitutional right to be sentenced before a sentencing circle or to seek other community participation during sentencing? Can the *Charter* be used to resist attempts by judges to consult local community members at sentencing? No reported cases have considered these questions, nor were they raised by any offender or counsel during the course of this study.

As all offenders sentenced through the sentencing circles considered appeared to have consented to this approach, use of the *Charter* as a shield against state oppression during circle sentencing seems unlikely. The *Charter*'s application will more likely be raised where an offender does not consent to some other form of community involvement in the sentencing process, or where community antagonism or lack of offender support has aggravated sentencing. Whether a right to involvement of an offender's local community in sentencing might be an Aboriginal right, protected by sections 25 and 35 of the *Charter,* remains a vital issue, but one that is outside the scope of this book. This question was not raised in any sentencing case considered.[34]

Despite the lack of judicial consideration of the *Charter* involving community sentencing, it has been applied in other sentencing cases. For example, in *Smith* v. *R.*[35] the mandatory seven-year sentence for importing narcotics under the *Narcotic Control Act* was invalidated as it was held to violate section 12 of the *Charter.* In *R.* v. *Wallace*[36] the lack of a local temporary absence program was found to deny the offender her right to equal protection and equal benefit under the law under section 15 of the *Charter,* resulting in the sentence of a fine rather than imprisonment. In *R.* v. *Willocks*[37] the Crown's refusal to divert a non-Aboriginal offender to an alternative-measures program for Aboriginal offenders was found not to constitute a breach of the offender's rights under section 15(1) of the *Charter.* More recently, Justice Noble of the Saskatchewan Court of Queen's Bench, in *Latimer,*[38] granted a constitutional exemption of the minimum sentence of life imprisonment with no chance of parole before ten years after Robert Latimer was convicted of second-degree murder. This was done on the basis that this sentence was grossly disproportionate in the circumstances and thereby constituted cruel and unusual punishment, contrary to section 12 of the *Charter.* The evidentiary basis for this ruling included the jury's recommendation that Latimer be eligible for parole after one year. Given the breadth of the cases mentioned, it is likely that the constitutional implications of community sentencing and mediation will be litigated at some point in the not-too-distant future.

Many factors will influence the development of community sentencing and mediation in Aboriginal communities and across the Canadian justice system as a whole. Conflicting views are sure to continue on key questions such as the range of offenders and offences that should be allowed to appear before community sentencing or mediation circles and the role of victims within these processes. These debates will contribute greatly to the evolution of Canadian justice policy as it relates to Aboriginal offenders, victims, and communities.

Policy Implications of Expanded Community Sentencing

The local initiatives studied were based in the conventional justice system but intersected with and related to, in varied fashion, local systems of social control and dispute resolution. Although judges may be considered by some Aboriginal people to be agents of state control, several judges presiding in the communities studied asserted their judicial independence in response to local community concerns and their own recognition of problems existing within the prevailing system. Judge Fafard was clearly conscious of the need for countering his court's lack of local credibility. He did this partly through his introduction of circle sentencing into the Aboriginal communities of northern Saskatchewan.

The community sentencing and mediation initiatives studied demonstrated a conjunctive relationship between local Aboriginal communities and the conventional Canadian justice system. Despite this conjunctive relationship, many Aboriginal people have envisaged breaking away from the prevailing system and establishing an independent justice and dispute-resolution system. CHCH assessment team member Marcel Hardesty of Hollow Water expressed the conviction that eventually his community would break from the prevailing justice system and operate independently. He said control and reform of offender behaviour would be achieved through public awareness of specific offenders and offences, and through education and treatment of offenders, suggesting that dispute resolution and social control would be dependant on local rather than central authority.[39]

The evolution of the community sentencing and mediation approaches considered in this study, whether moving towards total local autonomy within a separate justice system as advocated recently by the Royal Commission on Aboriginal Peoples[40] or simply towards increased local participation and control within the existing system, will depend on resolution of the justice issues raised in this book. In addressing these issues, the following courses of action will enhance the development and credibility of community sentencing and mediation.

1.   Recognition of approaches by appellate authority

Outside Saskatchewan, no appellate court has commented, in any depth, on the community sentencing approaches identified and analysed in this study. Within Saskatchewan, a significant difference of opinion on the breadth and applicability of circle sentencing is apparent in the majority and minority decisions in *Morin* and *Taylor*.[41] Although specific appellate guidelines should not be required, and perhaps are undesirable, appellate recognition and support of these approaches across Canada will be crucial to the continued evolution of community sentencing.

2.   Government support through provision of personnel and treatment facilities

Although the voluntary participation and support of community members is vital to the development of sentencing and mediation initiatives, expansion of government-funded resources, specifically providing trained personnel and treatment facilities, will be essential to the development and expansion of these approaches. Availability of these resources will increase the community-based sentencing options open for repeat offenders and will facilitate offender rehabilitation through community-based treatment and supervision. Governments must see a choice between funding these programs or continuing to pay currently high incarceration costs.

3.   *A focus on victim participation and support*

Despite an apparent concern by local community participants favouring victim involvement and support within the initiatives studied, a greater emphasis on voluntary participation by and organized support and protection for victims, both through formal justice channels and through local community involvement, will facilitate the development of initiatives. Enhanced support, protection, and voluntary participation will reduce the chances of victim alienation from the system, as well as promote healing by victims and reconciliation among victims, offenders, and local communities.

4.   *Protocol negotiation between local communities and justice system representatives*

Crown support is essential to the continuation and development of community sentencing and mediation. Although this support can be expressed in various forms, one way of ensuring ongoing support and consistency within these initiatives will be through the negotiation of protocols between local communities and representatives of the justice system. These will establish the conditions precedent to and the procedures to be followed within such community sentencing approaches.[42] Establishment of protocols will also ensure continuity of approach within each initiative and help reduce the dependence upon and the influence of any one individual in the development of initiatives.[43]

5.   *Development and expansion of criminal mediation*

Mediation was the only model studied that diverted full decision-making power from the prevailing system to local community members. Although the *Criminal Code* now formally recognizes alternative measures for adults, expansion of this approach, by diverting more offenders from the court system, will increase the amount of court time available for consideration of more serious charges.[44] At the same time, communities will be allowed to regain some measure of control over criminal dispute resolution. For expansion of mediation to be effective, training in mediation and facilitation skills should be provided to local committee members.

12 | Conclusion

Community sentencing and mediation initiatives in Canadian Aboriginal communities are in the initial stages of development. Judge Fafard, the major non-Aboriginal informant for this study, repeatedly urged that it was too early to draw any firm conclusions about the impact of the community sentencing initiatives. While respecting this limitation, Rupert Ross's comment is prophetic: "The cries for local control over community justice are growing."[1] The need for sentencing reform in Canadian Aboriginal communities is undeniable, if only because of highly disproportionate incarceration rates in the conventional system. It is to be hoped that this study has provided insight into the functioning and evolution of community sentencing and mediation in Aboriginal communities, and that it will generate discussion and debate about the appropriate path for future sentencing reform.

Local feelings of estrangement and separation from the Canadian justice system among Aboriginal people have recently come to co-exist with feelings of empowerment among local participants in community sentencing and mediation. In an apparent contradiction, these participants were prepared to devote considerable time and energy towards initiatives operating within a system they had frequently criticized. Their active involvement, however, suggested these initiatives were having a positive impact at the community level.

The breadth of discretion existing within the prevailing justice system has allowed judges and justice officials to adapt significantly the process and substance of sentencing in Aboriginal communities. Although the reforms considered in this study have not achieved an autonomous justice system for Aboriginal people, they do highlight the flexibility available within the conventional system to allow for a recognition of Aboriginal practices and processes, and to involve local community members in a sentencing process previously dominated solely by lawyers and judges.

The evolution of community sentencing and mediation may be deeply distressing to those who believe strongly in provincewide sentencing uniformity. Many of the sentences resulting from these approaches are outside established appellate sentencing ranges. Although sentencing uniformity is a concept innate to Canadian criminal law, blind adherence to this principle neglects the current reality in Aboriginal communities. As identified through this study, local resources, including informal systems of social control previously ignored by the conventional court system, are now being accessed by judges with a view towards promoting changed offender behaviour and increased public safety.

Local sentencing systems provide the potential for achieving the broader Canadian sentencing goals of deterrence, denunciation, and rehabilitation. Judge Stuart's analysis of the tension existing between community sentencing and principles of sentence uniformity is compelling:

> To fit the sentence to the circumstances not only of the offence and offender, but also to the needs of the victim and the community, and [to] do so within available time and resources requires significant information and time. The temptation to impose standard sentences must be overcome for the sentencing process to avoid squandering scarce resources, and to be used to its full potential in achieving its objectives.[2]

Most would agree that the ultimate goal of any criminal justice system is protection of the public. Given the obvious over-incarceration of Aboriginal people, even the possibility of these approaches succeeding, by changing offender behaviour and deterring crime, makes their continued development important, if not crucial.

A significant danger exists if such processes become forums for political interference and the persecution of unpopular or marginalized offenders or victims. Vigilance both by judges and community participants will be required to avoid this. If victims are to be directly involved in these approaches, care must be taken to ensure their support and protection, both during and after adjudication. Although the goal of public protection is laudable, these words are hollow if the developing processes lead to the alienation and re-victimization of victims.

The continuing evolution of these community-based approaches depends on a broad spectrum of support and participation, including local community members, judges, Crown and defence counsel, and probation officers. According to Associate Chief Judge Giesbrecht of the Provincial Court of Manitoba, the past two decades have seen other sentencing projects come and go in Aboriginal communities.[3] Their demise was usually brought about by the departure of a key participant. It is essential that the evolving initiatives not come to be controlled by any one individual or lobby group. A major strength of the approaches studied was that they enjoyed broad-based support both within local circles and the broader justice system.

Perhaps five years from now many answers will have been provided to the questions raised in this study. It is to be hoped that many of these answers will have been articulated by Aboriginal voices. Other questions will not have been answered and, indeed, may never be. If this study has accomplished anything, it will be to provide insights, particularly for the non-Aboriginal justice community, into the current reality of sentencing and mediation reform in Aboriginal communities and to offer some guidance towards the issues surrounding its continued development.

Notes

Introduction

1 T. Quigley, "Some Issues in Sentencing Aboriginal Offenders" in R. Gosse, J. Youngblood Henderson, & R. Carter, eds., *Continuing Poundmaker and Riel's Quest: Presentations Made at a Conference on Aboriginal Peoples and Jusice* (Saskatoon, Saskatchewan: Purich, 1994) 269 at 272–77.

2 [1995] 4 C.N.L.R. 37 (Sask. C.A.) at 72. Also cited at [1995] 9 W.W.R. 696, (1995) 134 Sask.R. 120, (1995) 101 C.C.C. (3d) 124, (1995) 42 C.R. (4th) 339.

3 M. Jackson, "Locking Up Natives in Canada" (1988–89) 23:2 U.B.C. L. Rev. 215 at 215.

4 Ibid. at 216.

5 Statistics Canada, Catalogue No. 85-211 at table 17.

6 Royal Commission on Aboriginal Peoples, *Bridging the Cultural Divide: A Report on Aboriginal People and Criminal Justice in Canada* (Ottawa: Queen's Printer, 1996) at 29.

7 (1996), 50 C.R. (4th) 326 (Yuk. Ter. Ct.) at 342–43.

Chapter 1

1 A. Mewett & M. Manning, *Mewett and Manning on Criminal Law*, 3d ed. (Toronto: Butterworths, 1994) at 3–4.

2 (1788), 100 Eng. Rep. 368 (K.B.) at 368.

3 J. H. Baker, *Introduction to English Legal History*, 3d ed. (London: Butterworths, 1990) at 570–71. Also see S. F. C. Milsom, *Historical Foundations of the Common Law*, 2d ed. (Toronto: Butterworths, 1981) at 406–15.

4 J. F. Stephen, *A General View of the Criminal Law of England* (1890; reprint, Colorado: Fred Rothman, 1985) at 9–18. Despite this central authority, pre-modern criminal trials in England were usually conducted locally and were often presided over by local lay justices of the peace, as noted by Milsom, *supra* chap. 1, note 3 at 414–15.

5 C. Harding & L. Koffman, *Sentencing and the Penal System: Text and Materials* (London: Sweet and Maxwell, 1988) at 81. Also see J. K. Jaffary, *Sentencing of Adults in Canada* (Toronto: University of Toronto, 1963) at 3.

6 V. G. Hines, *Judicial Discretion in Sentencing by Judges and Magistrates* (Chichester, England: Barry Rose, 1982) at #1-18.

7 J. H. Baker, *The Legal Profession and the Common Law: Historical Essays* (London: Hambeldon, 1986) at 292. This practice is reflected in the current right of a convicted offender to address the court prior to sentence under s. 726 of the *Criminal Code*.

8 Baker, *Intro. Eng. Hist.*, *supra* chap. 1, note 3 at 586–89.

9 Ibid. at 589–90. S. 748 of the *Criminal Code* still recognizes the power of Her Majesty or the Governor in Council to pardon a convicted offender.

10 As enshrined in English law by c. 29 of the *Magna Carta* (1225), enacted by

25 Edw. 1 (1297), which states, in part, that "no freeman shall be taken or imprisoned . . . but by lawful judgment of his peers."

11 Baker, *Intro. Eng. Hist., supra* chap. 1, note 3 at 590–91.

12 Law Reform Commission of Victoria, *Appendices; The Role of the Jury in Criminal Trials* (Background paper #1, November 1985) [unpublished] at 58.

13 Baker, *Intro. Eng. Hist., supra* chap. 1, note 3 at 591.

14 L. Radzinowicz, *A History of the English Criminal Law and Its Administration From 1750: The Movement for Reform 1750–1833* (New York: Macmillan, 1948) at 95.

15 See W. Jones, "Our Changing Jury System" (1931) 6:4 Notre Dame Lawyer 395 at 408. The power of English courts to imprison or fine jurors for perverse verdicts was terminated in 1670 by *Bushels Case* (1670), 6 State Trials 999, as cited in New South Wales Law Reform Commission, "The Jury in a Criminal Trial" (Discussion paper, Sydney, 1985) [unpublished] at 16.

16 M. Gleisser, *Juries and Justice* (New York: A. S. Barnes, 1968) at 39–41.

17 (1975), 20 C.C.C. (2d) 449, [1976] 1 S.C.R. 616, (1975) 53 D.L.R. (3d) 161, (1975) 4 N.R. 277, (1975) 30 C.R.N.S. 209 (S.C.C.).

18 (1997), 112 C.C.C. (3d) 193, [1997] 1 S.C.R. 217, (1997) 142 D.L.R. (4th) 577, (1977) 207 N.R. 215, [1997] 2 W.W.R. 525, (1997) 152 Sask.R. 1, (1997) 4 C.R. (5th) 1 (S.C.C.). A new trial was ordered by the Supreme Court of Canada after questions surfaced about questioning of the jury panel prior to the trial.

19 (1997), 121 C.C.C. (3d) 326, 12 C.R. (5th) 112.

20 Baker, *Intro. Eng. Hist., supra* chap. 1, note 3 at 583.

21 *Report of the Canadian Sentencing Commission: Sentencing Reform; A Canadian Approach* (Ottawa: Supply and Services Canada, February 1987) at 22.

22 Jaffary, *supra* chap. 1, note 5 at 10.

23 Canadian Sentencing Commission, *supra* chap. 1, note 21 at 24.

24 D. Thomas, *Principles of Sentencing: The Sentencing Policy of the Court of Appeal Criminal Division*, 2d ed. (London: Heinemann, 1979) at 6.

25 D. Thomas, *Constraints on Judgement: The Search for Structured Discretion in Sentencing, 1860–1910,* Institute of Criminology Occasional Series No. 4 (Cambridge, England: University of Cambridge, 1979) at 1.

26 24 & 25 Vict. 1861, cc. 94–100.

27 S.C. 1869, cc. 18–36.

28 Thomas, *Principles of Sentencing, supra* chap. 1, note 24 at 6.

29 Canadian Sentencing Commission, *supra* chap. 1, note 21 at 30.

30 Thomas, *Principles of Sentencing, supra* chap. 1, note 24 at 7. Also see Canadian Sentencing Commission, ibid. at 35.

31 L. Radzinowicz & R. Hood, *History of English Criminal Law: The Emergence of Penal Policy,* vol. 5 (London: Stevens & Sons, 1986) at 741–47.

32 Thomas, *Constraints on Judgement, supra.* chap. 1, note 25 at 47–74.

33 Jaffary, *supra* chap. 1, note 5 at 10–13. Also see discussion of the principle of deterrence in Radzinowicz & Hood, *supra* chap. 1, note 31 at 753 and in Thomas, *Constraints on Judgement, supra* chap. 1, note 25 at 49–52.

34 Canadian Sentencing Commission, *supra* chap. 1, note 21 at 31–32. Also see D. Brown, *The Genesis of the Canadian Criminal Code of 1892* (Toronto: Osgoode Society, 1989) at 23–26. The *Criminal Code* is currently cited as R.S.C. 1985, c. C-46.

35 See generally part XXXIII of the *Code* entitled "Sentencing."

36   R.S.C. 1985, c. Y-1. On May 12, 1998, federal justice minister Anne McLellan announced her government's intention to replace the *Young Offenders Act* with a new youth criminal justice act.

37   S. 20(k) provides a maximum disposition of three years for an offence, with a maximum penalty of life under the *Criminal Code*. S. 20(k.1) defines the maximum disposition for first- and second-degree murder.

38   Dickson J., in *R. v. Gardiner*, (1982), 68 C.C.C. (2d) 477 (S.C.C.) at 513–14, also cited at [1982] 2 S.C.R. 368, (1982) 140 D.L.R. (3d) 612, (1982) 43 N.R. 361, (1982) 30 C.R. (3d) 289, characterized the sentencing hearing as an exercise in which the sentencing judge seeks to obtain relevant and reliable information to shape the ultimate decision on disposition.

39   (1970), 1 C.C.C. (2d) 307 (Sask. C.A.) at 310–11. Also cited at (1970) 75 W.W.R. 644, (1970) 12 C.R.N.S. 392. See also the comments of Lane J.A. in *R. v. Jackson*, (1993), 87 C.C.C. (3d) 56 (Sask. C.A.) at 62–65. Also cited at [1994] 3 W.W.R. 125, (1993) 116 Sask.R. 146.

40   (1993), 81 C.C.C. (3d) 83 (Sask. C.A.) at 94–95. Also cited at 109 Sask.R. 8.

Chapter Two

1   Cumberland House also has a significant Metis community; however, a majority of the residents are treaty status Cree Indians who are either members of the Cumberland House Band or obtained their treaty status through *Bill C-31*.

2   Indian and Native Affairs Canada, *The Canadian Indian* (Ottawa: Supply and Services Canada, 1986) at 10.

3   See M. Coyle, "Traditional Indian Justice in Ontario: A Role for the Present?" (1986) 24 Osgoode Hall L. J. 605 at 612.

4   INAC, *supra* chap. 2, note 2 at 9–10. This contrasted with the agricultural-based tradition of the Iroquois to the south.

5   Coyle, *supra* chap. 2, note 3 at 612. For an anthropological history of the Western Woods Cree, see W. Sturtevant, *Handbook of North American Indians*, vol. 6 (Washington: Smithsonian Institute, 1981) at 217–30. Historical accounts of Ojibway culture are found in W. Warren, *History of the Ojibway People* (St. Paul: Minnesota Historical Society Press, 1984), and E. Danzinger, *The Chippewas of Lake Superior* (Norman, Oklahoma: University of Oklahoma Press, 1979). An account of the "ceremonies, rituals, songs, dances, prayers and legends" of the Ojibway is found in B. Johnson, *Ojibway Heritage* (Toronto: McClelland & Stewart, 1987).

6   Coyle, *supra* chap. 2, note 3 at 612–13.

7   R. McDonnell, "Contextualizing the Investigation of Customary Law in Contemporary Native Communities" (1992) 34 Can. J. Crim. 299 at 301. Also see E. J. Dickson-Gilmore, "Finding the Ways of the Ancestors: Cultural Change and the Invention of Tradition in the Development of Separate Legal Systems" (1992) 34 Can. J. Crim. 479 at 489–90.

8   Telephone interview with Judge Claude Fafard, September 19, 1995.

9   Dickson-Gilmore, *supra* chap. 2, note 7 at 481.

10   Public Inquiry into the Administration of Justice and Aboriginal People, *Report of the Aboriginal Justice Inquiry of Manitoba: The Justice System and Aboriginal People,* vol. 1 (Winnipeg: 1991) at 50.

11   D. Jenness, *The Indians of Canada*, Bul. 65 Anthr. Ser. No. 15 (Ottawa: Department of Mines, 1934) at 125.

12   Ibid.

13 AJI, *supra* chap. 2, note 10 at 22–23.
14 The interpretation of F. Jennings, *The Invasion of America* (New York: Norton & Co., 1975) at 111 was favoured by the commissioners as Jennings had sought to avoid stereotyping and cultural bias in presenting a more realistic, accurate, and fair version of history. Jennings' account, however, is based on the history of more southerly American Indian tribes.
15 AJI, *supra* chap. 2, note 10 at 53.
16 Coyle, *supra* chap. 2, note 3 at 615.
17 Ibid. at 622.
18 I. Hallowell, *Culture and Experience* (Prospect Heights, Illinois: Waveland Press, 1955) at 120.
19 AJI, *supra* chap. 2, note 10 at 51.
20 Ibid. at 52.
21 R. Ross, "Leaving Our White Eyes Behind: The Sentencing of Native Accused" [1989] 3 C.N.L.R. 1 at 7.
22 Ibid. at 8.
23 J. Milloy, *The Plains Cree: Trade Diplomacy and War: 1790 to 1870* (Winnipeg: University of Manitoba Press, 1988) at 79. The Plains Cree apparently share the traditional heritage of the Woodlands Cree, having moved onto the plains from the woodlands. D. Mandelbaum, "The Plains Cree Remembered" in *Proceedings of the Plains Cree Conference, October 24, 1979* (Regina, Saskatchewan: Canadian Plains Research Center, University of Regina) at 4–5.
24 D. Mandelbaum, *The Plains Cree: An Ethnographic, Historical and Comparative Study* (Regina: Canadian Plains Research Center, 1979) at 123.
25 Interview with Agnes Morin, November 16, 1994, Sandy Bay, Saskatchewan.
26 This practice among mid-nineteenth century Ojibway is described in F. Baraga, *Chippewa Indians* (New York: League of Slovenian Americans, 1976) at 24; and Warren, *supra* chap. 2, note 5 at 139. A similar practice among the Cree was described by Mandelbaum, *Ethnographic History, supra* chap. 2, note 24 at 122.
27 Mandelbaum, *Ethnographic History*, *supra* chap. 2, note 24 at 122, commented that "[a] payment of horses sometimes commuted blood vengeance."
28 A. Skinner, "Notes on the Plains Cree" (1914) 16 Am. Anthr. 68 at 72.
29 (1997), 122 C.C.C. (3d) 376 (Sask. C.A.).
30 Ibid. at 396. Also see *Saila* v. *R.,* [1984] N.W.T.R. 176 (N.W.T. Sup. Ct.), where de Weerdt J. upheld a probation order containing a condition of banishment.
31 J. Trudeau, *Culture Change Among the Swampy Cree Indians of Winsk, Ontario* (Ph.D. Thesis, Catholic University of America, 1966) at 23.
32 AJI, *supra* chap. 2, note 10 at 50–54. Also see Baraga, *supra* chap. 2, note 26 at 22, where the author wrote in the mid-nineteenth century of a form of community council among the Ojibway through which community members "deliberate[d] on some difficulties among themselves or some concerns with their traders etc."
33 Interview with Berma Bushie, February 6, 1995, Hollow Water, Manitoba.
34 Interview with Verna Merasty, October 20, 1994, Sandy Bay, Saskatchewan.
35 These are the dates used to circumscribe this era by historian Arthur Ray in *Indians in the Fur Trade: Their Role as Trappers, Hunters and Middlemen in the Lands Southwest of Hudson Bay: 1660–1870* (Toronto: University of Toronto Press, 1974).
36 Ibid. at xi.

37 Ibid.
38 R. Smandych & R. Linden, "Co-existing Forms of Aboriginal and Private Justice: An Historical Study of the Canadian West" in K. Hazelhurst, ed., *Legal Pluralism and the Colonial Legacy: Indigenous Experiences of Justice in Canada, Australia and New Zealand* (Aldershot, England: Avebury, 1995) 1 at 15.
39 Ibid. at 25.
40 P. Thistle, *Indian-European Trade Relations in the Lower Saskatchewan River Region to 1840* (Winnipeg: University of Manitoba Press, 1986) at 50–51.
41 Linden & Smandych, *supra* chap. 2, note 38 at 25.
42 AJI, *supra* chap. 2, note 10 at 58.
43 Ibid. at 59.
44 Ibid.
45 H. Hickerson, *The Chippewa and Their Neighbors: A Study in Ethnohistory* (Prospect Heights, Illinois: Waveland Press, 1987) at 13.
46 A. McMillan, *Native People and Cultures of Canada* (Vancouver: Douglas & McIntyre, 1988) at 145.
47 AJI, *supra* chap. 2, note 10 at 64.
48 R. Ross, *Dancing With a Ghost: Exploring Indian Reality* (Toronto: Octopus, 1992) at 103.

Chapter Three

1   AJI, *supra* chap. 2, note 10 at 22.
2   Ibid.
3   Interview with Harry Morin, October 19, 1994, Sandy Bay, Saskatchewan.
4   Community Holistic Circle Healing, *CHCH Position on Incarceration* (Hollow Water, Manitoba, 1993) [unpublished] at 4.
5   Department of Justice of Quebec, *Cree and Justice Symposium: Problematics on Justice in the Cree Milieu* (Prepared by the Consulting Services in Social Sciences, Development and Cultural Change SSDCC Inc. English version by the Department of Justice of Quebec) [unpublished] at 14.
6   L. Mandamim et al., "The Criminal Code and Aboriginal People" (1992) U.B.C. L. Rev. Special Edition 5 at 9.
7   M. Nielson, "Native People and the Criminal Justice System: The Role of the Native Courtworker" (1982) 5:1 Can. Legal Aid R. 55 at 56.
8   Law Reform Commission of Canada, *Report on Aboriginal Peoples and Criminal Justice: Equality, Respect* (Minister's Reference, Report 34, Ottawa 1991) at 6.
9   Task Force on the Criminal Justice System and Its Impact on the Indian and Metis People of Alberta, *Justice on Trial: Report of the Task Force on the Criminal Justice System and its Impact on the Indian and Metis People of Alberta (Canada)*, vol. 1 (Edmonton, Alberta: The Task Force, 1991) at 9-6.
10 Former director general of the Aboriginal Justice Initiative, Justice Canada, and subsequently deputy minister of Justice in the Northwest Territories, Don Avison previously practised as a defence lawyer and Crown counsel in the Yukon.
11 D. Avison, "Clearing Space: Diversion Projects Sentencing Circles and Restorative Justice" in R. Gosse, J. Youngblood Henderson, & R. Carter, eds., *Continuing Poundmaker and Riel's Quest: Presentations Made at a Conference on Aboriginal Peoples and Justice* (Saskatoon, Saskatchewan: Purich, 1994) 235 at 238.

12 Interview with Derek Custer & Cecile Merasty, October 20, 1994, Pelican Narrows, Saskatchewan.

13 N. Sibbeston, "Circuit Court: The Community's Perspective" (Presentation at the founding convention of The Northern Conference in March 1994 at Yellowknife) in *Circuit Court and Rural Court Justice in the North: A Resource Publication* (Vancouver: Simon Fraser University, 1985) at 1–6.

14 H. Morin interview, *supra* chap. 3, note 3.

15 C. Griffiths & S. Verdun-Jones, *Canadian Criminal Justice* (Toronto: Butterworths, 1989) at 751.

16 Interview with RCMP constable Brian Brennan, November 15, 1995, Sandy Bay, Saskatchewan.

17 C. Fafard, "On Being a Northern Judge" in R. Gosse, J. Youngblood Henderson, & R. Carter, eds., *Continuing Poundmaker and Riel's Quest: Presentations Made at a Conference on Aboriginal Peoples and Justice* (Saskatoon, Saskatchewan: Purich, 1994) 403 at 403–04.

18 Brennan interview, *supra* chap. 3, note 16.

19 Ibid.

20 *R.* v. *Bear* (Sask. Prov. Ct.) [unreported], hereafter called the "Sandy Bay circle."

21 Telephone interview with Judge Bria Huculak, October 12, 1994.

22 J. Batten, *Lawyers* (Toronto: Macmillan, 1980) at 117–18. The colourful career of this judge was also portrayed in J. Scissons, *Judge of the Far North: Memoirs of Jack Scissons* (Toronto: McClelland & Stewart, 1968).

23 Interview with Greg Bragstad, October 19, 1994, Sandy Bay, Saskatchewan.

24 Ross, "White Eyes," *supra* chap. 2, note 21 at 2.

25 M. Sinclair, "Aboriginal Peoples, Justice, and the Law" in R. Gosse, J. Youngblood Henderson, & R. Carter, eds., *Continuing Poundmaker and Riel's Quest: Presentations Made at a Conference of Aboriginal Peoples and Justice* (Saskatoon, Saskatchewan: Purich, 1994) 173 at 183–84.

26 Ross, "White Eyes," *supra* chap. 2, note 21 at 6.

27 Custer & Merasty interview, *supra* chap. 3, note 12.

28 *Report of the Saskatchewan Indian Justice Review Committee* (Regina 1992) at 43.

29 Hereinafter called the "Pelican Narrows circle."

30 Quigley, *supra* Intro., note 1 at 275.

Chapter Four

1 R.S.C. 1985, c. C-5 as amended.

2 R.S.C. 1985, c. Y-1 as amended.

3 S.C. 1996, c. 19.

4 (1992), 71 C.C.C. (3d) 347 (Yuk. Ter. Ct.) at 357. Also cited at [1992] 3 C.N.L.R. 116, (1992) 11 C.R. (4th) 357.

5 P. Nadin-Davis, *Sentencing in Canada* (Toronto: Carswell, 1982) at 513–14.

6 This was the conclusion drawn by Dickson J. in *Gardiner, supra* chap. 1, note 38 at 514.

7 (1962), 133 C.C.C. 57 at 62.

8 *Gardiner, supra* chap. 1, note 38 at 514. S. 724(3)(e) of the *Criminal Code* provides that "[t]he prosecutor must establish, by proof beyond a reasonable doubt, the existence of any aggravating fact or any previous conviction by the offender."

9   To obtain such a hearing, an offender must, after serving fifteen years of a life sentence for first-degree murder, apply to a superior court to be allowed a hearing to determine whether the number of years to parole should be reduced. See s. 745.61.

10   Interview with Ina Ray, November 15, 1994, Sandy Bay, Saskatchewan.

11   Pursuant to s. 20(1).

12   S. 11(7) of the act allows a young person who is not represented by a lawyer to ask the youth court judge to allow him or her to be represented by an adult who is deemed suitable by the judge.

13   S. 721(1) provides this report is to be prepared "in writing" by a probation officer. In *R. v. Webb* (1975), 28 C.C.C. (2d) 456, (1975) 9 Nfld. & P.E.I.R. 136, (1975) 39 C.R.N.S. 314 (P.E.I.S.C.), discussions between the judge and probation officer outside of court were held to be outside the scope of considerations permitted by this section.

14   A. MacAskill & H. Andrews, "The Role of the Youth Court Judge at the Disposition Hearing" (1985), 47 C.R. (3rd) 60 at 72–73.

15   See G. Parker, "Commentary on Criminal Law and Use of Pre-Sentence Report" (1964) 42 Can. Bar Rev. 621 at 627.

16   In s. 14(3).

17   "President's Task Force on Victims of Crime, Final Report VI" 1982, as reproduced in A. Klein, *Alternative Sentencing: A Practitioner's Guide* (Cincinnati: Anderson Publishing, 1988) at 137.

18   D. Sinclair et al., "Report of the Canadian Federal-Provincial Task Force on Justice for Victims of Crime" (1983), as quoted in D. Barfknecht, "Concerns of Canada's Victim's Rights Movement" (1985) 8 Cdn. Com. L.J. 83 at 83–84.

19   *Supra* chap. 4, note 17.

20   Standing Committee on Justice and Solicitor General on its Review of Sentencing, Conditional Release and Related Aspects of Corrections, *Taking Responsibility* (Ottawa: Queens Printer, 1988) at 18, who cited the opinion of Canadian victimologist Dr. Micheline Baril.

21   *Final Report: Safety Net; A National Conference on Crime Prevention, Public Safety and Justice Reform* (Burlington: CAVEAT, 1994) at 48.

22   S. Rosenfeldt & S. Sullivan, "Victims Rights: Discussion Paper" in *DNA Testing and the Law [and] Victims Rights* (Ottawa: Victims of Violence, 1994) at 5.

23   Klein, *supra* chap. 4, note 17 at 138.

24   *Supra* chap. 4, note 4 at 262.

25   A. Maron, "The Juvenile Diversion System in Action: Some Recommendations For Change" (1976) 22 Crime & Delinquency 461–69, cited in D. Fischer & R. Jeune, "Juvenile Diversion: A Process Analysis" (1987) 28:1 Cdn. Psych. 60 at 61.

26   K. Pate & D. Peachey, "Face to Face Mediation Under the Young Offenders Act" in J. Hudson, J. Hornick, & B. Burrows, eds., *Justice and the Young Offender in Canada* (Toronto: Wall & Thompson, 1988) at 105.

27   D. McGillis, "The American Resolution Dispute Movement" in *Mediation in the Justice System: Dispute Resolution Papers Series #2* (New York: American Bar Association, 1983) at 18–19.

28   *Supra* chap. 2, note 29 at 403.

29   See *Community Tribunals: A Community Sentencing Model: Final Draft Proposal* (Toronto: Operation Springboard, undated). The program description was taken from this proposal.

30 See *Aboriginal Legal Services of Toronto's Community Council Project* (Toronto 1992) [unpublished].

31 S. 718.3 establishes this discretion:
718.3(1) Where an enactment provides different degrees or kinds of punishment in respect of an offence, the punishment to be imposed is, subject to the limitation prescribed in the enactment, in the discretion of the court that convicts the person who commits the offence.

32 S. 267(1)(b).

33 E. Hall, "Sentencing the Individual" in B. Grossman, ed., *New Directions in Sentencing* (Toronto: Butterworths, 1980) 302 at 305.

34 C. Ruby, *Sentencing,* 4th ed. (Toronto: Butterworths, 1994) lists thirty-four factors affecting sentence in chap. 5. .

35 Quigley, *supra* Intro., note 1 at 277.

36 AJI, *supra* chap. 2, note 10 at 399.

37 These decisions are *R.* v. *Shropshire* (1995), 102 C.C.C. (3d) 193, [1995] 4 S.C.R. 227, (1995) 129 D.L.R. (4th) 657, (1995) 188 N.R. 284, (1995) 43 C.R. (4th) 269; *R.* v. *M.(C.A.)* (1996), 105 C.C.C. (3d) 327, [1996] 1 S.C.R. 500, (1996) 194 N.R. 321, (1996) 73 B.C.A.C. 81, (1996) 46 C.R. (4th) 269; and *R.* v. *McDonnell* (1997), 114 C.C.C. (3d) 436, [1997] 1 S.C.R. 948, (1997) 145 D.L.R. (4th) 577, (1997) 210 N.R. 241, [1997] 7 W.W.R. 44, (1997) 49 Alta.L.R. (3d) 111, (1997) 196 A.R. 321, (1997) 6 C.R. (5th) 231.

38 *Shropshire, supra,* chap. 4, note 37 at 209–10.

39 *Supra* chap. 4, note 37 at 374.

40 [1997] 117 C.C.C. (3d) 110 (Sask. C.A.).

41 At 123.

42 *Supra* chap. 4, note 37 at 374.

43 (1986), 26 C.C.C. (3d) 193 (N.W.T.C.A.).

44 *R.* v. *Sandercock* (1985), 22 C.C.C. (3d) 79, [1986] 1 W.W.R. 291, (1985) 40 Alta.L.R. (2d) 265, (1985) 62 A.R. 382, (1985) 48 C.R. (3rd) 154 (Alta. C.A.).

45 *Supra* chap. 4, note 43 at 198.

46 Telephone interview with Judge Claude Fafard, December 16, 1994.

47 L. Perreaux, "Band Dumps Justice Panel" Saskatoon *StarPhoenix* (March 5, 1997) A1.

48 L. Perreaux, "Indian Band Accused of Discrimination" Saskatoon *StarPhoenix* (March 6, 1997).

49 *R.* v. *H.K.C.* [1977] S.J. No. 577 (QL) (Sask. C.A.) and *R.* v. *S.W.M.* [1997] S.J. No. 574 (QL) (Sask. C.A.).

50 Quigley, *supra* Intro., note 1 at 292. Also see B. Archibald, "Sentencing and Visible Minorities: Equal and Affirmative Action in the Criminal Justice System" (1989) 12 Dalhousie L.J. 377.

51 Author's notes on Sandy Bay court, April 19, 1995.

52 Interview with Judge Robert Kopstein, May 31, 1995, Winnipeg, Manitoba.

53 R. Weninger, "Jury Sentencing in Noncapital Cases: A Case Study of El Paso County, Texas" (1994) 45 Wash. Univ. J. Urban Cont. L. 3.

54 See C. Reese, "Jury Sentencing in Texas: Time for a Change?" (1990) 31 South Texas L. Rev. 323 at 328, where these states are listed as Arkansas, Kentucky, Mississippi, Missouri, Oklahoma, Tennessee, Texas, and Virginia.

55 *Supra* chap. 1, note 19.

56 American Bar Association Project on Minimum Standards for Criminal Justice, *Standards Relating to Sentencing Alternatives and Procedures* (New York: American Bar Association, 1968) at 44.

57   See Note, "Jury Sentencing in Virginia" (1967) 53 Va. L. Rev. 968 at 970.
58   National Advisory Commission on Criminal Justice Standards and Goals, "The Courts: Task Force Report" (1973) in N. Kittrie & E. Zenoff, eds., *Sanctions, Sentencing, and Corrections* (New York: Foundation Press, 1981) at 65.
59   American Bar Association, *supra* chap. 4, note 56 at 45.
60   Ibid. at 46. See also "Virginia," *supra* chap. 4, note 57 at 978 and Note, "Statutory Structures for Sentencing Felons to Prison" (1960) 60 Colum. L. Rev. 1134 at 1156.
61   H. LaFont, "Assessment of Punishment—A Judge or Jury Function?" (1960) 38 Texas L. Rev. 835 at 843. Also see C. Kerr, "A Needed Reform in Criminal Procedure" (1918) 6 Kentucky L.J. 107 at 109.
62   American Bar Association, *supra* chap. 4, note 56 at 46.
63   Lafont, *supra* chap. 4, note 61 at 842.
64   C. Betts, "Jury Sentencing" (1956) 2 N.P.P.A.J. 369 at 371.
65   *Supra* chap. 4, note 4 at 360–61.
66   Not all offences have a victim who is clearly identifiable. For example, offences such as possession of a narcotic or impaired driving (without causing bodily harm to another person) have no identifiable victim other than, perhaps, the public at large. Realistically, no victim would be available for court purposes.
67   [1987] N.W.T.R. 1 (N.W.T.S.C.) at 11.
68   AJI, *supra* chap. 2, note 10 at 409.
69   Saskatchewan Indian Justice Review Committee, *supra* chap. 3, note 28.
70   (1991), 6 C.R. (4th) 126 (Yuk. Ter. Ct.) at 136. Also cited at [1991] N.W.T.R. 301
71   *R.* v. *D.N.* [1993] Y.J. No. 193 (QL) (Yuk. Ter. Ct.) at 31.
72   Interview with Donald McKay, Jr., December 13, 1994, Cumberland House, Saskatchewan.
73   Bragstad interview, *supra* chap. 3, note 23.
74   Interview with Cyril Roy, December 12, 1994, Cumberland House, Saskatchewan.
75   These included Rodney Garson of the Yukon, Pierre Rousseau of the Northwest Territories, Pierre Desrosiers of Quebec, Robin Ritter of Saskatchewan, George deMoissac of Manitoba, and Jim Langston of Alberta.
76   J. Bowers & P. Rousseau, *Workshop on the Role of Crown Counsel in an Aboriginal Context* (Draft report) [unpublished] at 3–7.

Chapter 5

1   *Supra* chap. 4, note 4.
2   Ibid. at 355–56.
3   Ibid. at 356.
4   Ibid. at 356–57.
5   *R.* v. *Thomas* (December 3, 1993), Kinistin Reserve (Sask. Prov. Ct.), which was the first sentencing circle within the Melfort area Provincial Court circuit. Judge Eric Diehl of the Provincial Court of Saskatchewan presided at the circle.
6   *R.* v. *C.S.*, Winnipeg (Man. Q.B.) [unreported], hereafter referred to as the "Winnipeg circle."
7   Robin Ritter was employed by the Saskatchewan Legal Aid Commission in La Ronge until February 1994 and is now employed by the Saskatchewan Depart-

ment of Justice as regional Crown prosecutor for northeast Saskatchewan.

8   R. Ritter, *Sentencing Circles* (La Ronge, Saskatchewan, 1993) [unpublished] at 2.

9   S. Davies, "Experiences with Circle Court" (Paper presented to the Northern Justice Society Conference in Kenora, Ontario, 1993) [unpublished].

10   Interview with Joyce Dalmyn, January 28, 1995, Winnipeg, Manitoba. At the time of this study, Joyce Dalmyn was employed as director of Manitoba Legal Aid in The Pas and had been active in the development of sentencing initiatives at Pukatawagan.

11   See B. Stuart, "Circles into Square Systems: Can Community Processes be Partnered with the Formal Justice System?" (Whitehorse, 1995) [unpublished] at 2.

12   *Supra* Intro., note 2.

13   Ibid. at 74.

14   *Supra* chap. 4, note 37 at 374.

15   (1994), 116 Nfld. & P.E.I.R. 293.

16   Ibid. at 297.

17   (1996), 177 N.B.R. (2d) 124 at 128.

18   (1995), 132 Sask.R. 221 (Sask. Q.B.) at 224. Also cited at [1995] 3 C.N.L.R. 167.

19   *Supra* chap. 2, note 29 at 408.

20   *Supra* chap. 4, note 4 at 356.

21   Judge Dutil was the first judge to introduce sentencing circles into northern Quebec and the presiding judge in two reported sentencing circle cases, *R.* v. *Aluka* (1993), 112 D.L.R. (4d) 732; and *R.* v. *Naappaluk*, [1994] 2 C.N.L.R. 143.

22   M. Nemeth, "Circle of Justice: Northern Villagers Take Part in Sentencing" *Maclean's* (September 19, 1994) at 52.

23   *Supra* Intro., note 2 at 48.

24   (1995), A.R. 238 (Alta. C.A.) at 6.

25   *Supra* chap. 5, note 17 at 135.

26   *Supra* chap. 5, note 21.

27   M. Crnkovich, "Report on the Sentencing Circle in Kangiqsujuaq" in *Inuit Women and Justice,* Progress Report #1 (Ottawa: Pauktuutit Inuit Women's Association, undated) at 21.

28   *R.* v. *Whitecap* (October 10, 1997) Red Earth, Saskatchewan (Sask. Prov. Ct.) [unreported].

29   Fafard interview, *supra* chap. 4, note 46.

30   Ritter, *supra* chap. 5, note 8 at 2.

31   (1993) 114 Sask.R. 2, [1994] 1 C.N.L.R. 150 (Sask. Q.B.).

32   Interview with RCMP constable Murray Bartley, December 14, 1994, Cumberland House, Saskatchewan.

33   Brennan interview, *supra* chap. 3, note 16.

34   S*upra* Intro., note 2 at 75.

35   (1994), 24 W.C.B. (2d) 114 (Yuk.Ter. C.A.).

36   This passage was taken from the case summary. More recently, Prowse J.A. of the same court echoed these concerns in *R.* v. *Johns* [1996] 1 C.N.L.R. 172 (Yuk. Ter. C.A.) at 178 (also cited at 66 B.C.A.C. 97, 17 M.V.R. (3d) 251):
In my view, however, circle sentencing is no longer in its embryonic stages, particularly in the Yukon and in the northern parts of this province. That being

so, further heed must be paid to the recommendation of [this court] in the *R. v. Johnson* . . . that rules or alternatively, well-publicized guidelines for circle sentencing, should be established by Territorial Court judges, with the assistance of those with expertise in the process.

37 Bartley interview, *supra* chap. 5, note 32.

38 [1995] 6 W.W.R. 438 (Sask. Prov. Ct.) at 442–46.

39 Ibid. at 439.

40 *Supra* chap. 5, note 17.

41 *Supra* chap. 5, note 31 at 152.

42 *Supra* chap. 5, note 21 at 735–38.

43 *Supra* Intro., note 2.

44 Ibid. at 46.

45 *Supra* chap. 5, note 38 at 442.

46 *Supra* chap. 2, note 29.

47 Ibid. at 401.

48 Ibid. This case has continued to draw attention as the offender recently appeared in a Saskatoon court charged with sexual assault and assault causing bodily harm; however, charges were subsequently stayed. See Saskatoon *StarPhoenix,* April 19, 1998, A3, and June 18, 1998, A3.

49 Kopstein interview, *supra* chap. 4, note 52.

50 [1994] Y.J. No. 107 (QL) at 3.

51 Brennan interview, *supra* chap. 3, note 16.

52 Protocol of the Katapamisuak Society at the Poundmaker Cree Nation in Saskatchewan (North Battleford, 1993) [unpublished].

53 *Supra* chap. 5, note 38.

54 Protocol for Manitoba Department of Justice Support for the Community Approach of the Hollow Water Community Holistic Circle Healing (Brandon, Manitoba, 1991) [unpublished].

55 *R.* v. *Manyfingers,* [1996] 191 A.R. 342.

56 *R.* v. *Webb,* [1993] 1 C.N.L.R. 148 (Yuk. Ter. Ct.); *R.* v. *Charleboy,* [1993] B.C.D. Crim. Sent. 7100–06 (B.C. Prov. Ct.); and *R.* v. *C.P.,* [1995] Y.J. No. 186 (QL) (Yuk. Ter. Ct.).

57 *Morin, supra* Intro., note 2.

58 *D.N., supra* chap. 4, note 71; *C.S., supra* chap. 5, note 6 (although, in this case, the judge did not accept the recommendation of the sentencing circle); and *Taylor, supra* chap. 2, note 29. See the discussion later in this chapter respecting circle sentencing of child sexual assault cases at Hollow Water, Manitoba.

59 *Naappaluk, supra* chap. 5, note 21.

60 *Gingell, supra* Intro., note 7.

61 *R.* v. *Rope* (1994), 136 Sask.R. 167, (1994), 17 M.V.R. (3d) 262 (Sask. Q.B.). The sentence resulting from this circle was upheld on appeal at [1995] 4 C.N.L.R. 98 (Sask. C.A.).

62 *Nicholas, supra* chap. 5, note 17.

63 *Thomas, supra* chap. 5, note 5.

64 *Aluka, supra* chap. 5, note 21.

65 (1993), 80 C.C.C. (3d) 143 (Sask.Q.B.) at 149–50.

66 *Supra* Intro., note 2.

67 Ibid. at 47.

68 *Supra* chap. 4, note 4 at 370.

69 An approach established by the Alberta Court of Appeal in *Sandercock, supra* chap. 4, note 44.

70 *Supra* Intro., note 1 at 290.
71 *Supra* chap. 5, note 17 at 136.
72 *Supra* chap. 4, note 37 at 446–53.
73 See M. Shaffer, "Divorce Mediation: A Feminist Perspective" (1988) 46:1 U.T. Fac. L. Rev. 162 at 182.
74 Crnkovich, *supra* chap. 5, note 27 at 24.
75 Telephone interview with Rupert Ross, January 4, 1995.
76 Ibid.
77 Interview with Associate Chief Judge Murray Sinclair, January 17, 1995, Winnipeg, Manitoba.
78 (1991), 120 A.R. 106 (Alta. C.A.).
79 [1996] 3 W.W.R. 88.
80 Ross interview, *supra* chap. 5, note 75.
81 *Supra* Intro, note 2.
82 J. Campbell, "Morin Says Sentence Was Just" *New Breed Magazine* (May 1993) 3 at 4.
83 M. Miller, "Forgiveness Replaces Blame: Sentencing Circle Experiment in Saskatoon" (1993) 13:1 St. Thomas More College Newsletter 4 at 5.
84 (1994) 35 C.R. (4th) 55 at 59–60. Also cited at [1995] 2 C.N.L.R. 151.
85 *Morrissette, supra* chap. 1, note 39 at 310–11.
86 [1994] Y.J. No. 47 (QL) (Yuk. Ter. Ct.) at 3.
87 CHCH, *supra*, chap. 3, note 4 at 2–3.
88 Bushie interview, *supra* chap. 2, note 33.
89 *Supra* chap. 4, note 71 at para. 34.
90 Bragstad interview, *supra* chap. 3, note 23.
91 J. Braithwaite, *Crime, Shame and Reintegration* (Cambridge: Cambridge University Press, 1989) at 54–68.
92 (1982), 8 W.C.B. 197 (Sask. C.A.).
93 This information was provided by INAC.
94 Bushie interview, *supra* chap. 2, note 33. CHCH deals with offenders and victims from Hollow Water and the three Metis communities.
95 Field trips to Hollow Water were conducted February 6 and 22, 1995. Data collected included interviews with CHCH assessment team members and Judge Murray Sinclair of the Provincial Court; observations of a community sentence review conducted February 22, 1995; discussions with community members at the review; and written material provided through CHCH, INAC, the Solicitor General of Canada, and assorted newspapers.
96 Rupert Ross, "Duelling Paradigms? Western Criminal Justice Versus Aboriginal Community Healing" in R. Gosse, J. Youngblood Henderson, & R. Carter, eds., *Continuing Poundmaker and Riel's Quest: Presentations Made at a Conference on Aboriginal Peoples and Justice* (Saskatoon, Saskatchewan: Purich, 1994) 241 at 243. These figures confirm the cycle of violence as some of the abusers must have been previously victimized.
97 Bushie interview, *supra* chap. 2, note 33.
98 Interview with Lorne Hagel, January 23, 1995, Winnipeg, Manitoba.
99 T. Lajeunesse, *Community Holistic Circle Healing: Hollow Water First Nation* (Ottawa: Solicitor General Canada, 1993) in appendix A.
100 Bushie interview, *supra* chap. 2, note 33.
101 Ibid.
102 Ibid.
103 [1989] M.J. No. 273 (QL) (Man. Prov. Ct.).

104 Community Holistic Circle Healing, CHCH *Position on Healing* (Hollow Water, . Manitoba, 1993) [unpublished] at 3–4.

105 Interview with Marcel Hardesty, February 22, 1995, Hollow Water, Manitoba.

106 Hagel interview, *supra* chap. 5, note 98.

107 *Supra* chap. 5, note 54.

108 Bushie interview, *supra* chap. 2, note 33.

109 K. Rollason, "Ceremony Heralds Healing: Ancient, Modern Ways Meet in Native Justice Venture" *Winnipeg Free Press* (December 11, 1993) A15. This circle is hereafter called the "Hollow Water circle."

110 Sinclair interview, *supra* chap. 5, note 77.

111 Community Holistic Circle Healing, *The Sentencing Circle* (Hollow Water, .Manitoba, 1993) [unpublished] at 3–4. This submission also recommended at 5–10: appropriate circle participants, community preparation for the sentencing circle, physical setting of the circle, and the process and rules to govern the circle. These recommendations appear to have been adopted by Judge Sinclair. See "Trial by Healing Circle" *Canadian Lawyer* March, 1994 at 7–8.

112 Sinclair interview, *supra* chap. 5, note 77.

113 Rollason, "Ceremony Heralds," *supra* chap. 5, note 109.

114 Sinclair interview, *supra* chap. 5, note 77.

115 P. Moon, "Native Healing Helps Abusers: Offenders Admit Guilt, Avoid Jail Terms" *The Globe and Mail* (April 8, 1995) A1 and A5.

116 Radio interview with Berma Bushie, *Afternoon Edition,* Canadian Broadcasting Corporation, January 12, 1995.

117 Bushie interview, *supra* chap. 2, note 33.

118 Hereafter called the "Hollow Water review."

119 Bushie interview, *supra* chap. 2, note 33.

120 Ibid.

121 Hardesty interview, *supra* chap. 5, note 105.

122 Bushie interview, *supra* chap. 2, note 33.

123 Because of s. 731(1)(b) of the *Criminal Code,* a probation order cannot follow a penitentiary term of over two years.

124 Interview with George deMoissac, June 29, 1995, Winnipeg, Manitoba.

125 "Trial by Healing Circle," *supra* chap. 5, note 111.

126 Ibid.

127 Ibid.

128 Bushie interview, supra chap. 2, note 33.

129 K. Goulet, "Oral History as an Authentic and Credible Research Base for Curriculum: The Cree of Sandy Bay and Hydroelectric Power Development 1927–67" (M.Ed. Thesis, University of Regina, 1986) at 80.

130 Ibid.

131 L. Morin, *The People of Wasawakasik* (Papyrus Printing, 1992) in chap. 1.

132 Ibid.

133 Goulet, *supra* chap. 5, note 129 at 79.

134 Ibid.

135 A. Morin interview, *supra* chap. 2, note 25.

136 Ray interview, *supra* chap. 4, note 10.

137 Field trips were conducted to Sandy Bay October 18–20 and November 12–17, 1994, and April 18–20, 1995. Data collected included observations of Provincial Court, the community-at-large, and interviews with community members and court party members involved with the sentencing initiatives. Written in-

formation was also obtained through INAC, the libraries at the University of Manitoba, and the Government of Saskatchewan.

138 H. Morin October interview, *supra* chap. 3, note 3.

139 Memorandum to file by Sid Robinson, July 27, 1992.

140 Memorandum to file by Sid Robinson, August 20, 1992.

141 Although no official record of the circles has been kept, Harry Morin estimated, on September 19, 1994, that nineteen or twenty sentencing circles had been conducted. Defence counsel Felicia Daunt, counsel to the first Sandy Bay circle, estimated, on September 28, 1994, that twenty sentencing circles had been held in Sandy Bay. Judge Fafard, when contacted on September 19, 1994, mentioned that often a number of offenders were dealt with in one sentencing circle and that his estimate of the total offenders dealt with in Sandy Bay sentencing circles was twenty.

142 This information was provided by RCMP constable Brian Brennan of Sandy Bay, who represented the RCMP at several Sandy Bay sentencing circles.

143 H. Morin October interview, *supra* chap. 3, note 3.

144 Brennan interview, *supra* chap. 3, note 16.

145 Those interviewed were predominately persons involved in either the youth sentencing advisory committee or circle sentencing.

146 H. Morin October interview, *supra* chap. 3, note 3.

147 Merasty interview, *supra* chap. 2, note 34.

148 Bragstad interview, *supra* chap. 3, note 23.

149 H. Morin October interview, *supra* chap. 3, note 3.

150 Ibid.

151 Bragstad interview, *supra* chap. 3, note 23.

152 Ray interview, *supra* chap. 4, note 10.

153 Fafard December interview, *supra* chap. 4, note 46.

154 See this discussion in chap. 5 regarding criteria for circle sentencing.

155 Fafard December interview, *supra* chap. 4, note 46.

156 Following the Sandy Bay circle, the Crown appealed the suspended sentence given to the offender on a charge of assault against his spouse.

157 Fafard December interview, *supra* chap. 4, note 46.

158 Ibid.

159 Ibid.

160 Huculak October interview, *supra* chap. 3, note 21.

161 Telephone interview with Sid Robinson, February 17, 1995.

162 Brennan interview, *supra* chap. 3, note 16.

163 Ibid.

164 Telephone interview with Diane Christianson, October 21, 1994.

165 In one case, she indicated the victim was opposed to a sentencing circle. This was reported to the court and Judge Fafard declined the request.

Chapter 6

1 Law Reform Commission of Canada, "The Principles of Sentencing and Dispositions" (Working Paper No. 3, 1974) at 29, as cited in S. Zimmerman, "The Revolving Door of Despair: Aboriginal Involvement in the Criminal Justice System" (1992) U.B.C. Law Rev. (Special Ed.: Aboriginal Justice) 367 at 386.

2 Law Reform Commission of Canada, *supra* chap. 3, note 8.

3 Ross, *Dancing With Ghost*, *supra* chap. 2, note 48 at 167.

4   *Supra* chap. 4, note 70 at 128.
5   Also see S. Yaeger, "Circle Sentencing Programs Give Yukon Indian Bands an Alternative to Traditional Legal System" *The Lawyers Weekly,* October 1, 1993, at 12.
6   Dalmyn interview, *supra* chap. 5, note 10. The justice committee involved a mixture of elders and younger community members.
7   Interview with Judge William Martin, April 11, 1995, The Pas, Manitoba.
8   Dalmyn interview, *supra* chap. 5, note 10.
9   Ibid.
10 Lay assessors have been used in British admiralty courts and other tribunals. These are persons with special knowledge or expertise who sit with and assist judges. Zimmerman, *supra* chap. 6, note 1 at 386.
11 *Supra* chap. 5, note 28.
12 Kopstein interview *supra* chap. 4, note 52.
13 L. Longclaws, L. Barkwell, & P. Rosebush, "Research Note: Report of the Waywayseecappo First Nation Domestic Violence Project" (1994) XIV:2 Can. J. Nat. St. 341 at 343.
14 Information on Waywayseecappo was obtained from INAC in Winnipeg.
15 This detachment's area includes Waywayseecappo.
16 A field trip was conducted to Waywayseecappo on March 2, 1995. Data collected included observations of court conducted March 2, 1995, and interviews with members of the Elders Justice Advisory Council, Judge Giesbrecht, the local probation officer, a band councillor in charge of justice matters, an RCMP sergeant from Rossburn, and defence and Crown counsel. Written information was also obtained from INAC.
17 Telephone interview Judge Brian Giesbrecht, February 24, 1995.
18 Interview with Associate Chief Judge Brian Giesbrecht, March 2, 1995, Waywayseecappo First Nation, Manitoba.
19 Interview with Herman Mentuck, March 2, 1995, Waywayseecappo First Nation, Manitoba.
20 Telephone interview with band councillor Tim Cloud, March 9, 1995.
21 On March 2, 1995, this included meeting before court to discuss some of the cases to be dealt with that day.
22 Mentuck interview, *supra* chap. 6, note 19.
23 Ibid.
24 Giesbrecht interview, *supra* chap. 6, note 17.
25 Telephone interview with Merv Hart, June 8, 1995, Brandon, Manitoba.

Chapter 7

1   *Supra* chap. 5, note 15 at 298. In this case, the court rejected the request for a sentencing circle on the basis that the victim did not feel she could participate as she had not yet healed.
2   Ibid. at 299.
3   C. Fafard, "Address to the Fifth Northern Conference, Sitka, Alaska, April 1991" in C. T. Griffiths, ed., *Self-Sufficiency in Northern Justice Issues* (Vancouver: Simon Fraser University, 1992) at 270–71.
4   H. Morin October interview, *supra* chap. 3, note 3.
5   Ray interview, *supra* chap. 4, note 10.
6   Fafard December interview, *supra* chap. 4, note 46.

7   Interview with Derek Custer, November 16, 1995, Pelican Narrows, Saskatchewan.
8   Ibid.
9   Interview with Judge Claude Fafard, November 14, 1994, Pelican Narrows, Saskatchewan.
10 Fafard December interview, *supra* chap. 4, note 46.
11 Telephone interview Judge Claude Fafard, September 19, 1994.
12 Fafard December interview, *supra* chap. 4, note 46.
13 Information provided by INAC.
14 Fafard December interview, *supra* chap. 4, note 46.
15 Custer interview, *supra* chap. 7, note 7.
16 Ibid.
17 Interview with RCMP corporal Bob MacMillan, November 16, 1994, Pelican Narrows, Saskatchewan.
18 Custer interview, *supra* chap. 7, note 7.
19 Merasty & Custer interview, *supra* chap. 3, note 12.
20 Fafard November interview, *supra* chap. 7, note 9.
21 Ibid.
22 Fafard December interview, *supra* chap. 4, note 46.
23 Telephone interview with Judge Bria Huculak, December 7, 1994.
24 MacMillan interview, *supra* chap. 7, note 17.
25 Ibid.
26 Telephone interview with Cathy Bohachik, June 28, 1995.

Chapter Eight

1   This is described in detail by Lilles T.C.J. in *Gingell, supra* Intro., note 7.
2   This is described in detail by Jacobson P.C.J. in *Manyfingers, supra* chap. 5, note 55.
3   Interview with RCMP corporal Kirke Hopkins, April 18, 1995, Pelican Narrows, Saskatchewan.
4   Jackson, "Locking Up Natives," *supra* Intro., note 3 at 277.
5   Law Reform Commission of Canada, "Studies on Diversion" (Working Paper No. 7, 1975), as cited in M. Jackson, "In Search of Pathways to Justice: Alternative Dispute Resolution in Aboriginal Communities" (1992) U.B.C. L. Rev. (Special Ed.: Aboriginal Justice) 147 at 178.
6   McKay interview, *supra* chap. 4, note 72.
7   Roy interview, *supra* chap. 4, note 74.
8   Bartley interview, *supra* chap. 5, note 32.
9   MacMillan interview, *supra* chap. 7, note 17.
10 Huculak December interview, *supra* chap. 7, note 23. Judge Huculak is now a resident judge in Saskatoon.
11 Bartley interview, *supra* chap. 5, note 32.
12 McKay interview, *supra* chap. 4, note 72.
13 Huculak December interview, *supra* chap. 7, note 23.
14 C. Fafard, *Sentencing Circle: A Progress Report* (La Ronge, Saskatchewan, undated) [unpublished].
15 Information obtained from INAC.
16 Interview with RCMP corporal Robert Brossart, April 11, 1995, Pukatawagan, Manitoba. A field trip was conducted to Pukatawagan from April 9–12, 1995.

Data collected respecting this community included observations of court held April 11, interviews with the local justice committee, defence counsel Joyce Dalmyn, RCMP corporal Robert Brossart, probation officer Karen Dumas, and Judge William Martin. Other written materials respecting Pukatawagan were obtained through the justice committee, INAC, and the libraries at the University of Manitoba.

17 Interview with Gabriel Bighetty, April 10, 1995, Pukatawagan, Manitoba.
18 B. Lowery, "Local Native Officials Tame North's Dodge City" *Winnipeg Free Press* (November 16, 1992) B3.
19 Interview with Hy Colomb, April 10, 1995, Pukatawagan, Manitoba.
20 Dalmyn interview, *supra* chap 5, note 10.
21 G. York, *The Dispossessed: Life and Death in Native Canada* (Toronto: Lester & Orpen Dennys, 1989) at 170.
22 Dalmyn interview, *supra* chap. 5, note 10.
23 H. Colomb interview, *supra* chap. 8, note 19.
24 Interview with Liz Bear, April 10, 1995, Pukatawagan, Manitoba.
25 Brossart interview *supra* chap. 8, note 16.
26 Ibid.
27 Bear interview, *supra* chap. 8, note 24.
28 H. Colomb interview, *supra* chap. 8, note 19.
29 G. Bighetty interview, *supra* chap. 8, note 17.
30 Bear interview, *supra* chap. 8, note 24.
31 Interview with George Colomb, April 10, 1995, Pukatawagan, Manitoba.
32 Brossart interview, *supra* chap. 8, note 16.
33 Dalymn interview, *supra* chap. 5, note 10.
34 Brossart interview, *supra* chap. 8, note 16.
35 G. Bighetty interview, *supra* chap. 8, note 17.
36 Bear interview, *supra* chap. 8, note 24.
37 Ibid.
38 Martin interview, *supra* chap. 6, note 7.
39 Ibid.
40 Brossart interview, *supra* chap. 8, note 16.
41 Ibid.
42 Dalmyn interview, *supra* chap. 5, note 10.
43 Interview with Karen Dumas, April 11, 1995, Pukatawagan, Manitoba.

Chapter 9

1 *Supra* chap. 2, note 29.
2 See H. Astor, "Swimming Against the Tide: Keeping Violent Men Out of Mediation" in *Women, Male Violence and the Law* (Sydney: Institute of Criminology, 1994) at 147.
3 Bushie interview, *supra* chap. 2, note 33.
4 Merasty interview, *supra* chap. 2, note 34.
5 Dalmyn interview, *supra* chap. 5, note 10.
6 Author's notes, Sandy Bay circle, April 19, 1995.
7 Brossart interview, *supra* chap. 8, note 16.
8 W. Goulding, "Sentencing Circle Used Previously By Suspect," Saskatoon *StarPhoenix* (June 6, 1995) A6, which focussed on the previous circle sentencing experience of person arrested on a charge of break and enter.

9   Stuart, *supra* chap. 5, note 11 at 5.
10 McKay interview, *supra* chap. 4, note 72.
11 *Supra* chap. 5, note 38 at 445.
12 Dalmyn interview, *supra* chap. 5, note 10; and Brossart interview, *supra* chap. 8, note 16.
13 This victim had recently been sentenced to custody and was also experiencing further medical problems resulting from the assault being considered in the sentencing circle.
14 Roy interview, *supra* chap. 4, note 74.
15 Interview with Felicia Daunt, April 19, 1995, Sandy Bay, Saskatchewan.

Chapter 10

1   P. Fitzpatrick, "Crime As Resistance: The Colonial Situation" (1989) 28:4 Howard J. 272 at 276.
2   S. Merry, "Law and Colonialism" (1991) 25:4 Law & Soc. Rev. 889 at 894.
3   R. Smandych & G. Lee, "Women, Colonization and Resistance: Elements of an Amerindian Autohistorical Approach to the Study of Law and Colonialism" (1995) 10:1 Native Studies Rev. 21 at 24–26.
4   R. Kidder, "Toward an Integrated Theory of Imposed Law" in S. Burman & B. Harrell-Bond, eds., *The Imposition of Law* (New York: Academic Press, 1979) at 293.
5   M. Brogden, "Law and Criminal Labels: The Case of the French Metis in Western Canada" (1990) 1:2 J. Human Just. 13.
6   Merry, *supra* chap. 10, note 2 at 919.
7   See G. Prakash, "Postcolonial Criticism and Indian Historiography" (1992) 31–32 Social Text 8, in which the author described and attacked the Eurocentric nature of many accounts of Indian history. Also see G. Spivak, "Three Women's Texts and a Critique of Imperialism" (1985) 12 Critical Inquiry 243, in which the author critiqued the imperialistic nature of nineteenth-century British literature through the eyes of a Third World person; and H. Bhabha, "Signs Taken for Wonders: Questions of Ambivalence and Authority Under a Tree Outside Delhi" (1985) 12 Critical Inquiry 144, in which the author described the role of English literature in colonization and the resulting forms of resistance to this. Other examples of post-colonial scholarship by Indigenous writers are A. Allahr, "When Black First Became Worth Less" (1993) 34:1-2 Int'l J. Comp. Soc. 39; and F. Mellon, "The Promise and Dilemma of Subaltern Studies: Perspectives from Latin America History" (1994) 99:5 Am. Hist. Rev. 1491.
8   Merry, *supra* chap. 10, note 2 at 906.
9   S. Ortner, "Resistance and the Problem of Ethnographic Refusal" (1995) 37:1 Comparative Studies Soc. & Hist. 173 at 190–91.
10 Merasty & Custer interview, *supra* chap. 3, note 12.
11 MacMillan interview, *supra* chap. 7, note 17.
12 Bear interview, *supra* chap. 8, note 24.
13 F. Snyder, "Colonization and Legal Form: The Creation of 'Customary Law' in Senegal" (1981) 19 Journal of Legal Pluralism 49. Also see, Robert Gordon, "The White Man's Burden: Ersatz Customary Law and Internal Pacification in South Africa" (1989) 2:1 Journal of Historical Sociology 41, which traced the recreation of "customary law" within the apartheid system and argued this adoption can best be seen as an instrument of the "internal pacification" of the

Indigenous population.
14   S. Merry, "Legal Pluralism" (1988) 22 Law & Soc. Rev. 869 at 870.
15   S. Henry, "The Construction and Deconstruction of Social Control: Thoughts on the Discursive Production of State Law and Private Justice" in J. Lowman, R. Menzies, & T. Palys, eds., *Transcarceration: Essays in the Sociology of Social Control* (Aldershot: Gower Publishing, 1987) 89 at 90.
16   D. Black, *The Behaviour of Law* (New York: Academic Press, 1976) at 6–7 and 107–11.
17   Ibid. at 108–09.
18   R. Ellickson, *Order Without Law: How Neighbors Settle Disputes* (Boston, Massachusetts: Harvard University Press, 1991) at 282.
19   Ibid. at 283. Also see S. Henry, *Private Justice: Towards Integrated Theorising in the Sociology of Law* (London: Routledge & Kegan Paul, 1983), who described the development of "private law" systems of social control within workplaces.
20   Rupert Ross, "Cultural Blindness and the Justice System in Remote Native Communities" (Paper presented to the Sharing Common Ground Conference on Aboriginal Policing Services, Edmonton, May 1990) [unpublished] at 11–12, cited in M. Jackson, "In Search of the Pathways to Justice: Alternative Dispute Resolution in Aboriginal Communities" (1992) U.B.C. L. Rev. (Special Ed.: Aboriginal Justice) 147 at 208–09.
21   Sinclair interview, *supra* chap. 5, note 77.
22   *R.* v. *Dusomme* (1993) Winnipeg (Man. Prov. Ct.) [unreported].
23   Ross, "Duelling Paradigms?" *supra* chap. 5, note 96 at 241–43.
24   "Unlocking Aboriginal Justice: Alternate Dispute Resolution for the Gitksan and Wet'suwet'en People" (Proposal to the B.C. Minister of the Attorney General) [unpublished] at 15–19, as reproduced in M. Jackson, "In Search of the Pathways to Justice: Alternative Dispute Resolution in Aboriginal Communities" (1992) U.B.C. L. Rev. (Special Ed.: Aboriginal Justice) 147 at 210.
25   S. Merry, "Sorting Out Popular Justice" in S. Merry & N. Milner, eds., *The Possibility of Popular Justice: A Case Study of Community Justice in the United States* (Michigan: University of Michigan Press, 1993) 31 at 32.
26   Ibid. at 37. A criminal justice framework stressing victim/offender reconciliation and compensation, as opposed to offender punishment, was presented by criminologist Herman Bianchi in *Justice As Sanctuary: Toward of New System of Crime Control* (Indianapolis: Indiana University Press, 1994).
27   Merry, "Popular Justice," *supra* chap. 10, note 25 at 35.
28   P. Fitzpatrick, "The Impossibility of Popular Justice" in Merry & Milner, *supra* chap. 10, note 25 at 453.
29   Merry, "Popular Justice," *supra* chap. 10, note 25 at 40.
30   Ibid.
31   Ibid. at 42.
32   Ibid. at 45.
33   Ibid.

Chapter Eleven

1   Telephone interview with Judge Barry Stuart, September 18, 1994. Circle sentencing has been used regularly in the Yukon since 1992. See Nemeth, *supra* chap. 5, note 22.
2   Fafard December interview, *supra* chap. 4, note 46.

3   Stuart, *supra* chap. 5, note 11 at 14.

4   *Supra* chap. 5, note 38 at 443.

5   Giesbrecht J., *The Fatal Inquiries Act: Report by Provincial Court Judge Into the Death of Lester Norman Desjarlais* (Brandon, Manitoba, 1992) [unpublished] at 210.

6   Ibid. at 213. Also see A. McGillivray, "Therapies of Freedom: The Coloniza-tion of Aboriginal Childhood" in *Governing Childhood,* A. McGillivray, ed. (Aldershot, England: Dartmouth Press, 1996), for examples of political inter-ference with the operation of on-reserve child welfare agencies.

7   W. Gaylin, *Partial Justice: A Study of Bias in Sentencing* (New York: Alfred Knopf, 1974). In chap. 3 of this book, the author explores the personal biases held by individual judges, which, in turn, affected their decisions on sentence.

8   Dalmyn interview, *supra* chap. 5, note 10.

9   (1991), 15 W.C.B. (2d) 28 (B.C.C.A.).

10   This quote is from the case summary.

11   See T. Marshall, *Alternatives to Criminal Courts: The Potential for Non-Judi-cial Dispute Settlement* (Aldershot, England: Gower, 1985) at 10.

12   Interview with Theresa Bighetty, April 10, 1995, Pukatawagan, Manitoba.

13   Interview with Harry Morin, April 18, 1995, Sandy Bay, Saskatchewan.

14   Sentencing circles considered during this study involved a minimum of two and a maximum of fourteen hours.

15   *Supra* Intro., note 2.

16   MacMillan interview, *supra* chap. 7, note 17.

17   *R.* v. *Bogdan* (September 11, 1996) Katepwa (Sask. Prov. Ct.) [unreported]. See T. Sutter, "Circle Deals with Non-native Offender" *The Regina Leader-Post* (September 12, 1996) A6.

18   *R.* v. *Williamson* (June 3, 1997) Loon Lake (Sask. Prov. Ct.) [unreported]. See T. Coulombe, "Suspended Sentence in Accidental Death" *The Meadow Lake Progress* (June 8, 1997).

19   Ss. 718.2(d) and (e) of the *Code* also require that sanctions other than impris-onment, where appropriate or reasonable, be considered, with particular atten-tion to the circumstances of Aboriginal offenders.

20   In ss. 717–717.4. See chap. 4 for a full discussion of the statutory framework in the *Criminal Code* and the *Young Offenders Act* as each relates to community and victim participation in sentencing and in mediation/diversion.

21   (1998), 121 C.C.C. (3d) 504 (Alta. C.A.)

22   Ibid. at 524.

23   *Supra* Intro., note 2.

24   *Supra* chap. 2, note 29.

25   Provincial appellate courts in the Yukon (in *Johnson, supra* chap. 5, note 35) and Alberta (in *John, supra* chap. 5, note 24) have considered sentence appeals from lower court sentencing circles but have focussed on the fitness of sentence and have not commented at any length on the appropriateness of circle sentenc-ing or other forms of community sentencing.

26   It was undisputed at the appeal that the normal appellate range for the offence in question (robbery of a convenience store) would include a penitentiary term.

27   *Morin, supra* Intro., note 2 at 72.

28   *Supra* chap. 5, note 56 at 2–5.

29   *Supra* chap. 2, note 29 at 409.

30   Ibid. at 403.

31   See M. Mandryk, "Sentence Method Defended" *The Regina Leader-Post* (April

13, 1995) A8, where Opposition Justice critic Don Toth was said to have suggested that sentencing circles might be creating a two-tiered justice system granting "special treatment under the law based on race."

32 CHCH, *supra* chap. 3, note 4 at 3–4.

33 Enacted by *Canada Act 1982* (U.K.), c. 11.

34 The Supreme Court of Canada in *R.* v. *Van der Peet,* [1996] 2 S.C.R. 507, (1996) 137 D.L.R. (4th) 289, (1996) 200 N.R. 1, [1996] 9 W.W.R. 1, (1996) 23 B.C.L.R. (3d) 1, (1996) 109 C.C.C. (3d) 1, [1996] 4 C.N.L.R. 177, (1996) 50 C.R. (4th) 1, did consider, at length, the meaning of an "aboriginal right" in the context of a claim that a provincial fishing regulation was invalid because it violated s. 35(1) of the *Charter.* This analysis, however, was limited to the application of a provincial statute as opposed to the federal *Criminal Code.*

35 (1987), 34 C.C.C. (3d) 97, [1987] 1 S.C.R. 1045, (1987) 40 D.L.R. (4th) 435, (1987) 75 N.R. 321, [1987] 5 W.W.R. 1, (1987) 15 B.C.L.R. (2d) 273, (1987) 58 C.R. (3d) 193, (1987) 31 C.R.R. 193 (S.C.C.).

36 [1987] O.J. No. 1502 [QL] (Ont. Dist. Ct.).

37 [1994] 1 C.N.L.R. 167, 14 C.R.R. (2d) 373 (Ont. Ct. Just. Prov. Div.).

38 *Supra* chap. 1, note 19.

39 Hardesty interview, *supra* chap. 5, note 105.

40 *Supra* Intro., note 6 at 76–81.

41 *Supra* Intro., note 2 and chap. 2, note 29. In *Morin,* the offender had applied for leave to appeal his sentence to the Supreme Court of Canada but subsequently abandoned his application.

42 An example was the protocol signed between Hollow Water and the Manitoba Department of Justice in 1991.

43 One of the reasons the community of Hollow Water sought to negotiate a protocol with the Department of Justice was that Crown attorneys responsible for this community frequently changed, forcing the CHCH assessment team to re-educate each successive attorney.

44 Regardless of statutory recognition, the Crown still controls the range and number of offenders and offences to be diverted. The *Young Offenders Act* also allows young persons to be diverted from the court system through alternative measures.

Chapter Twelve

1 Ross "Cultural Blindness," *supra* chap. 10, note 20.

2 *R.* v. *N. (D.)* (1993), 27 C.R. (4th) 114 (Yuk. Ter. Ct.) at 126–27.

3 Giesbrecht interview, *supra* chap. 6, note 17.

Index